Higgins – 85
86
87 ✓
88
89
90
91
92

MW01001213

Higgins – 85
86
87 ✓

EVOLUTION OF THE
BICYCLE

Volume 2

Edited by:
Neil S. Wood

© Copyright 1994

ISBN# 0-89538-069-2

L-W Book Sales
P.O. Box 69
Gas City, IN 46933

Layout and Design by David Devon Dilley

© Copyright 1994
L-W Book Sales

Published by:
L-W Book Sales
P.O. Box 69
Gas City, IN 46933

ISBN# 0-89538-069-2

All rights reserved. No part of this publication may be reproduced, stored in a retrieval system, or transmitted in any form or by any means, electronic, mechanical, photocopying, recording or otherwise, without prior permission of the copyright owner or the publisher.

Table of Contents

Acknowledgements

We would like to thank everyone who helped out with this second volume of Evolution of the Bicycle. For those of you who were patient in waiting for this second volume we appreciate all of your patience. The people listed below are all that contributed to this book. If we missed anyone we would like to thank them for all of their help. We would like to give a special thank to Steve Castelli, without his help we would have been lost. Congratulations to everyone who contributed to the first book, without the first volume there would not have been a second volume. We would like to thank everyone again who sent us pictures and information. If we could not use your picture because of quality or some other reason, we are truly sorry. We also had a few problems reading some addresses and hope we came up with the correct information. If we did make an error regarding your bicycle information, please accept our apology.

Contributors
COLLECTORS, DEALERS & RESTORERS

Adams, Lionel – PO Box 284, Peshastin, WA 98847
Agan, Jim – 1057 58th Street, Des Moines, IA 50311
Agnew, Victor – 11320 Truman Rd., Independence, MO 64050
Albert, Ray – 170A Spahr-Seiling Rd. #2, Dillsburg, PA 17019
Allen, George W., Pedal Pusher – 233 Penner Drive, Pearl, MS 39208
Allen, James E. & Jamie – Rt. 10, Box 935-38, Springfield, MO 65803
Beale, Elery L. – 148 Water Street, Hallowell, ME 04347
Blansett, Irene – Alba, MO
Blum, Jim M. – 2228 N. 60th Street, Omaha, NE 68104
Branche, Walter – 452 S. Lakewood Ave., Ocoee, FL 34761-2726
Cafaro, Patric – 121 Holmes Drive, Fairborn, OH 45324
Carroll, Joe "Blackie" – 511 Bryden Ave., Lewiston, ID 83501
Carter, Steve & Carolyn – 559 Gibbs Street, Plainfield, IN 46168
Castelli, Steve – PO Box 559, Windsor, CA 95492
Cook, Chuck – 2254 Linden Drive, Salina, KS 67401
Cook, Ken – 2221 Cooper, Sheboygan, WI 53083
Cruz, Paul – 2268 W. Stockton Ave., Anaheim, CA 92801
Curcio, Gary – 537 Burritt St., New Britain, CT 06053-2823
Cutkomp, Ty – 33 Oak Lane, Davenport, IA 52803
Cycle Art – 2590 Pioneer Ave., Suite A, Vista, CA 92083-8427
Dahlquist, Daniel – 7636 Carden Drive, Radford, VA 24141-8852
Daniels, Ray – Springfield, MO 65803
DeDontney, Gary – 1385 Ranchita Drive, Los Altos, CA 94024
Dizer, John T. & William – 10332 Ridgecrest Rd., Utica, NY 13502
Doan, Steve – 506 2nd Ave. SW, Independence, IA 50644
Dr. Spokes Cyclery – 240 S. Center, Casper, WY 82601
Esch, Laurie A. – 33830 Glenview, Farmington, MI 48335
Fallon, Michael, Copake Country Auction – Box H, Copake, NY 12516
Fast, Larry D. – 2039 Summit Ave. NW, Salem, OR 97304
Figatner, Bill – 7706 Vine Street, River Forest, IL 60305
Fisher, Charlie & Courtney – 1262 Hawthorne Drive E., Wantash, NY 11793
Fitzgerald, Dan – 717 W. Stratford, Peoria, IL 61614
Floyd, Gene W. – 2207 S. Keller, Kennewick, WA 99337
Frising, Nic, Nancy & Billy, The Old Bicycle Shoppe – 519 Main St., Joplin, MO 64801
Gallagher, James T. – 15 Whitney Place, Saratoga Springs, NY 12866
Gandolfo, Quas – 5 Evergreen Drive, Seaville, NJ 08230
Ghamo, Romeo & Michael Johnson – 5324 Windward Drive, Erie, PA 16505
Golden, Jim – Erie, PA 16505
Gordon, John C. – PO Box 1948, Aspen, CO 81612
Gray, Craig – 13425 Dunrobin Ave., Bellflower, CA 90706
Griffin, Richard – 3625 Emery Rd., Adrian, MI 49221
Grimshaw, Paul R. – 21238 Cass Rd., Farmington Hills, MI 48335-5218
Guilford, Brad – 509 Whitten Ave., Hicksville, OH 43526
Hampton, Regis – 12831 Holloway Rd., Tampa, FL 33625-3831
Harper, Ray – 6381 Larkspur Drive, Mobile, AL 36619

Harton, Bob & Marianne – PO Box 535, Lansing, IL 60438

Harvieux, J. – 13716 Wellington Crescent, Burnsville, MN 55337

Helfand, Larry – 167 N. 9th St., Brooklyn, NY 11211

Holder, Kerry – 4064 Northwood Drive, Springfield, MO 65003

Hoss, James N., Barr Bicycle & Fitness – 1710 NW 86th Street, Des Moines, IA 50325

Huenink, Dirk – 4315 N. Bayshore Drive, Sturgeon Bay, WI 54235

Jennings, Dale R. – 1157 Sycamore Lane, Richmond, IN 47374

Jensen, Don – 411 4th Ave., N., Humbolt, IA 50548

Jew, Eddie – 460 Grand Ridge Pl., Monterey Park, CA 91754

Kaplan, Michael, Bowden Industries, Inc. – PO Box 3546, Lawrence, KS 66046

Kaplan, Michael, Hudson General Store – 18 Main Street, Hudson, MA 01749

Kinsey, Alan – 318 N.E. Grant, Ankeny, IA 50021-1810

Kizer, Greg, The Bike Shop – 10724 Thimler Rd., Grabill, IN 46741

Lauer, Wally & Meghan – 28063 Gratiot, Roseville, MI 48066

LeDoux, Ken – 1725 Sara St., Sulphur, LA 70663

Lepro, Dan – 12025 Cochise Cir., Conifer, CO 80433

Licon, Ralph, Tina, Danielle & Leandra – 2381 #A Beach St., Oceano, CA 93445

Little, Jerrell – 107 Deer St., Boone, NC 28607

Magee, Ken & Marta – 7751 N. 8th, Fresno, CA 93720

Mathre, Charles D., American Indian Motorcycle Co., Inc. – 486 Rich Gulch Rd., Mokelumne Hill, CA 95245

Matthews, M.T. – PO Box 1105, West Monroe, LA 71294

Meyer, Jeff – 1531 So. 19th, Lincoln, NE 68502

Meyers, Jeff – 6530 Leonard Drive, Harrisburg, PA 17111

Mueller, Peggy – 432 Mill Street, Long Lake, MN 55356

Muellner, Terry – 8507 Center, River Grove, IL 60171

National Bicycle History Archive – Box 28242, Santa Ana, CA 92799

Ohrt, Dave – 1519 No. 3rd St., Clinton, IA 52732

Olsen, Kent – 240 S. Center, Casper, WY 82601

Olson, Denis – 332 Niagara, Park Forest, IL 60466

Osman, Ken – 619 Hampshire Rd., Dayton, OH 45419

Palos, Laszlo – 109 Ruxton Ave., Manitou Springs, CO 80829

Parsons, Eric R. – 4266 Troost Ave., Studio City, CA 91604

Pearson, A.G. – 2343 Hwy. 49 S., Mariposa, CA 95338

Peoples, Jesse W. – R. 3, Box 252, Carrollton, IL 62016

Popp, Paul – PO Box 7000-45, Redondo Beach, CA 90277

Poyneer, Jim, The Selector – Rd. #5, Box 467, Oswego, NM 13126

Ratliff, Brad – 6026 Darkwood, Houston, TX 77088

Rhymers, Sherm & Donna – 5413 Newton Ave. So., Minneapolis, MN 55419

Riach, Mike, Dee, Dustin, Darrell & Tonya – 5724 W. Angela Dr., Glendale, AZ 85308

Rick – 90 E. Escalon #109, Fresno, CA 93710

Roscoe, Chris & Ian – 5811 N. 42nd St., Omaha, NE 68111

Rose, Al – 1711 W. 11th Street, Upland, CA 91786

Rosensweig, Hugh – 403 Lafayette Ave., Cincinnati, OH 45220

Roth, George – 341 Baileyville Rd., Middlefield, CT 06455

Rothenberger, James A. – 22 Pershing Ave., Lebanon, PA 17042

Ruffing, Mike, Mike's Bikes – 338 N. Niagara St., Burbank, CA 91505

Scheideman, Ollie H., 1215 Plumas St., Suite 201, Yaba City, CA 95991

Selders, Steve – 11999 Troy Dr., Baton Rouge, LA 70811

Siler, Herschel, The Country Studio – Hwy. 704, Rt. 4, So. Boston, Va 24592

Spangler, Ray – 128 Crandell Court, Schaumburg, IL 60193

Spillane, Jim – 85 Nortontown Rd., Madison, CT 06443

Townson, Charles – 22292 Pineville Rd., Pass Christian, MS 39571

Turner, Jerry, Nostalgic Reflections – PO Box 350, Veradale, WA 99037

Vaillancourt, Alan L. – 5441 N. Black Canyon, Phoenix, AZ 85015

Valosen, Nelson, NV'D Cycles – 27 Robbins Way, Southampton, NJ 08088

Vaughn, Donald S. – 221 Ridge Dr., Carlisle, PA 17013

Vallick, John – 13496 W. northern, Glendale, AZ 85307

Valtzer, Bill – 110 Greene St., New York, NY 10012

Veiler, Dave – 215 S. Park St., Kewanee, IL 61443

Ventzell, Alan – 708 Willmar St., Racine, WI 53402

West, Richard – 116 South 2nd Street, Richmond, IN 47374

Introduction

Bicycle collecting has grown in the past few years to an almost unbelievable proportion. I is one of the most desirable, fastest appreciating collectibles to be found today. It is now an adult toy.

We are not attempting to put out a book that will be a standard of the industry. This book has been published for your enjoyment and to help further the interest in Bicycle Collecting. I am sure some errors will be found in identification and pricing due to so many people working on this project. But again we hope you will enjoy it and further your education on your pursuit of the bicycle hobby.

Thank You,

Neil S. Wood, Editor
Scott A. Wood, Asst. Editor

L-W Book Sales
P.O. Box 69
Gas City, IN 46933

Pricing Information

The Price Guide in this book is for bicycles in good to excellent condition. Bicycles found with parts missing, very poor paint, wheels changed from originals or excessive rust will bring much lower prices. A bicycle considered to be in good condition is one with original paint and no parts missing. A bicycle in excellent condition is one that is 70% to 95% mint. This price guide is based on bicycles in these conditions. L-W Books can not be responsible for gains or losses, as this is ONLY A GUIDE.

The bicycles in this book have been priced by their owners, so you must realize that **ALL** prices are negotiable.

Places to Go - Reading to Do

Following are shows you don't want to miss if you are interested in Bicycles, Pedal Cars and related items.

Dayton, Ohio M.C.T.A. Show, April & October
Info: M.C.T.A., P.O. Box 403 N.D. Station, Dayton, OH 45404, Phone: 513-233-8381

Antique Toy & Doll World, St. Charles, IL, April, June & October
Info: Antique World Shows, Inc., P.O. Box 34509, Chicago, IL 60634
Phone: 312-725-0633

INDY ANTIQUE ADVERTISING SHOW, Indiana St. Fairgrounds, Indianapolis
March, June & September
Info: Mary Kokles, 6018 Northaven, Dallas, TX 75230
Phone: 214-240-1987

Brimfield, Mass. Shows in May, July & September
Phone: 413-245-3436

Annual Arkansas Pedal Car & Antique Toy Show & Sale, Memorial Day Weekend
Statehouse Convention Center, Little Rock, Arkansas
Info: Boy Toys Inc., 17916 B Interstate 30, Benton, AR 72015
Phone: Buzz Sawyer (501) 835-8498 Even. or Bill B. Hampton (501) 778-4604 Days

Greenville, SC Pedal Car & Toy Show, Memorial Weekend
Phone: 803-244-4308

VMBC Annual Meet, 2nd Weekend in July, Portland, IN
Info: John Martin, P.O. Box 62, Montpelier, IN 47359

Ann Arbor Swap Meet, April
Info: Classic Bicycle & Whizzer Club, 35768 Simon, Fraser, MI 48026

Hershey, Pennsylvania, National AACA Meet, October

Kalamazoo, MI, Antique Toy Circus Maximus, 3rd Saturday in May, Saturday after Thanksgiving
Info: 1720 Rupert, Grand Rapids, MI 49505
Phone: 616-361-9887

Taylor, MI, Antique Bicycles, Vintage Motor Bikes, Pedal Car Show, Toy Show and Swap Meet,
Every year in March
Info: JP Promotions, 9432 Sylvester, Taylor, MI, 48180
Phone: 313-849-1313, 11AM - 6PM, 313-295-0464, 5:30PM - 11PM

f you deal in Bicycles, Pedal Cars or related items, the following publications will be of interest to you.

he Bike Shopper, 1102 Greene St., Adel, IA 50003
Vheel Goods Trader, P.O. Box 435, Fraser, MI 48026
Vheelmen Newsletter, 14920 Garfield, Allen Park, MI 48101
Antique Trader, P.O. Box 1050, Dubuque, IA 52001
Antique Toy World, P.O. Box 34509, Chicago, IL 60634
Austin J-40 Car Club Newsletter, Mr. Brian Swann, 19 Lavender Ave., Coundon, Coventry, CV6 1DA, England
he Selector, R.R. #5 - Box 467, Oswego, New York 13126
he Pedal Pusher, 233 Penner Drive, Pearl, MS 39208
he Antique Classic Bicycle News, P.O. Box 1049, Ann Arbor, MI 48106
he Classic Bike Trader, 5546 Northland Rd., Indianapolis, IN 46208
he West Coaster, 7935 S. E. Market, Portland, Oregon, 97125
orth American Directory of Classic Bicycle Collectors & Dealers, Joan Truett, Arjay Communications,
     325 West Hornbeam Dr., Longwood, Florida 32779 (This has a listing of dealers, collectors,
     parts suppliers, restorers, shows and publications)
American Bicyclist Magazine, 400 Skokie Blvd., Suite 395, Northbrook, IL 60062-7903

Balloon Tire Bicycles

Collector of
Balloon Tire Bicycles
from the 30's, 40's & 50's
Buy — Sell — Trade

Gary De Dontney   415/962-1920

Wanted:
Bicycles

Made Before 1960
ALSO PARTS - TOOLS - ACCESSORIES

Dave Weiler   (309) 853-1902
215 S. Park Street   Kewanee, IL 61443

Buyer of Balloon Tire Bikes
Mens or Womens Models
Also Buying Incomplete Bikes
Parts Tools & Related Items

Mike's Bikes

Schwinn

BUY - SELL
TRADE - REPAIR
REFURBISH - RENT

338 N. NIAGARA ST., BURBANK, CA 91505
(818) 563 3020

James N. Hoss

BICYCLE AND FITNESS

Serving Des Moines Since 1920

1710 NW 86th St.
Des Moines, Iowa 50325   (515) 223-6111

HIGHEST PRICES PAID
FOR OLD BICYCLES   (708) 895-4165

Spoke - N - Memories
CLASSIC BICYCLES BOUGHT & SOLD

P.O. Box 535   Owners
Lansing, IL 60438   BOB & MARIANNE HARTON

Buying Old Bicycles
and Toys
From 1860's to 1960
• Parts • Literature • Advertising

TOYS...Tin wind ups, planes, motorcycles,
robots, character toys made in USA, Japan
or Germany.
ALSO BUYING...Pedal cars, whizzers, scooters
and motorcycles, parts and literature.

Dave Ohrt
Clinton, Iowa -- 319-243-8175

JIM SPILLANE

Collector of Bicycle Memorabilia

85 NORTONTOWN ROAD
MADISON, CONNECTICUT 06443   203/245-0080

WANTED
Rare and Unusual
Bicycles

FROM 1920 THRU 1950
Also
Advertising Literature
Signs & Parts

JAMES A. ROTHENBERGER
22 Pershing Avenue • Lebanon, PA 17042 • 717-273-2359

Vintage Bicycles

BOB NICHOLS
Carmel Valley, CA

Buy • Sell • Trade
(408) 659-2548

NOSTALGIC BICYCLES

CARTER
STEVE & CAROLYN
559 GIBBS ST.
PLAINFIELD, IN U.S.A.
46168

317-839-1621

Collector of Old Bicycles
Memorabilia • Parts
Restorations • Parades

Buy - Sell - Trade

Old Balloon
TIRED BIKES

ANTIQUES

STEVE DOAN
(319) 334-4100

506 2nd Ave. S.W.
Independence, IA 50644

WANTED

Pedal Cars • Trucks • Boats • Airplanes • Trains

J. HARVIEUX
13716 Wellington Crescent
Burnsville, MN 55337
(612) 890-4586

CyclArt

Since 1976

2590 'A' Pioneer Ave., Vista, CA 92083
619-599-1015 FAX 619-599-1017

James F. Cunningham
CyclArtist

Custom or Production Painting
Custom Graphics
Titanium Anodizing
Frame Repair and Modification
Classic Bicycle Restoration
Logo and Tradename Creation
OEM Graphics & Color Specification
Paintshop Performance Consulting

Call Today!

THE OLD BICYCLE SHOPPE

PURVEYORS OF ALL SORTS OF WHEELED CONTRIVANCES AND PARTS FOR SAME~ SPECIALIZING IN BALLOON TIRE BICYCLES....
LOCATED AT 519 MAIN STREET JOPLIN, MISSOURI 64801
TELEPHONE 417 781-6688
PROPRIETOR~ Nic Frising

NATIONAL BICYCLE HISTORY ARCHIVE
of America

Box 28242
Santa Ana, California
U.S.A.   92799
(714) 647-1949

Dedicated to preservation and enjoyment of old bicycles, memorabilia and bicycle history.

Contact: Leon Dixon, Curator
(714) 647-1949

Nostalgic Reflections
CUSTOM ETCHED PLATES
Jerry M. Turner
(509) 226-3522
P. O. BOX 350, VERADALE, WASHINGTON 99037

We make acid etched bicycle badges and decals for the bike collectors and restorers. These are made exactly like the originals.

We also make custom dash plaques, serial plates, instrument faces, decals, door sill plates, radiator scripts, porcelain medallions and clockfaces for antique cars, airplanes, motorcycles, bicycles and boats.

No job is too small. Many of our orders are one of a kind. We specialize in the "Hard to Find" or rare items.

If you have an original that you want reproduced, you must send us your original for our inspection. This will tell us how much art work is involved and what materials, thickness and etch depth is needed for reproduction. Then we send you a quote as to the cost involved.

We return all original items to their owners upon completion or quote refusal.

Call or write today with your needs. S.A.S.E.

Nostalgic Reflections
P.O. Box 350
Veradale, Washington
U.S.A.   99037
(509) 226-3522

Kerry Holder
35 Years Experience
Dealer*Appraiser*Auctioneer

4 Semi-Annual Auctions
1st Weekend Feb. - Nashville, TN
1st Weekend May - Springfield, MO
*New Auction in September in Springfield, MO
2nd Weekend Nov. - Springfield, MO
Also Estate Auctions

Pedal Cars, Bicycles, Motorcycles, Toys, Carousel Animals, Slots & Anything of Unusual Character

Rt. 20, Box 245
Springfield, MO 65803
Phone (417) 833-9439

WANTED
EARLY BICYCLES
Bicycles 1850-1950
THROUGH BALLOON

Related Memorabila:
advertising, art, books,
& toys, medals, trophies,
photos, posters, prints
etc.

COPAKE
AUCTION

Box H Copake, NY 12516
Phone 518-329-1142

Dr. Spokes Cyclery

The Best Deals on Two Wheels

Kent Olsen
Phone (307) 265-7740

240 S. Center
Casper, WY 82601

Dealer - Collector - Admirer

**Specializing in High Wheel Bicycles,
Motorcycles and Motor Bicycles
Also League of American Wheelman
(L.A.W.) memorabilia**

**Ty Cutkomp
Don't hesitate to call:**
(319) 323-7263

**33 Oak Lane
Davenport, IA 52803**

Collector – Rider

*Antique Bikes,
Accessories
&
Literature Wanted*

Paul R. Grimshaw
21238 Cass Road
Farmington Hills, MI 48335-5218

WANTED
EARLY BICYCLES
THROUGH BALLON BICYCLES: ALSO
RELATED ADVERTISING, MEMORABILA,
EPHEMERA, MEDALS, TROPHIES,
PHOTOS, TOYS, ORIGINAL ART,
POSTERS, PRINTS, BOOKS, ETC.

**Walter Branche
452 S. Lakewood Ave.
Ocoee, FL 34761-2726
Phone: (407) 656-4224**

WANTED
ANTIQUE - 1880-1890's - TURN OF CENTURY
BICYCLES
& Related Items

Including: High Wheel Bicycles;
Photographs; Paintings; Medallions;
Bicycle Parts; Lamps; Bells; And ???

Peggy Mueller

432 Mill Street
Long Lake, MN 55356

DAY: 612 473-0101   *EVE*: 612 476-1058

FAX: 612 476-6815

HUDSON GENERAL STORE
Antiques & Collectibles
WE BUY-SELL-TRADE
CASH FOR THE UNUSUAL

*pedal cars - old toys - bicycles - robots - vintage lace
- clothing - glass - pottery - jewelry -
advertising signs & tins - neons - victoriana - deco -
mission furniture & furnishings - country store items*

**Also Buying Estates - Attics - Old Store Stock -
Oak Display Cases
Collelctions - Single Items**

At The Rotary Jct Rts 62 & 85
508-562-5220

*Open By Chance Or By Appointment
Please Call Ahead
Outside Massachusetts 1-800-551-7767*

Michael Kaplan   **18 Main Street**
Luann Kaplan   **Hudson, MA 01749**

John C. Gordon
P.O. Box 1948
Aspen, CO 81612
Phone: (303) 925-7433

Bicycle Collector
■ ■ ■ ■ ■ ■ ■ ■ ■ ■ ■
CHUCK COOK
I Buy Old Bicycles

2254 Linden Dr. / Salina, KS 67401
H# **913-827-5884**

Wholesale & Retail
Books on Antiques & Collectibles

Over 600 titles
Write or call for FREE catalog:
L-W Book Sales
P.O. Box 69
Gas City, IN 46933

Vintage Motor Bike Club

National Club for Out of Production Motor Bikes & Scooters

For Membership Contact:
FREDERICK D. HIRSCH
VINTAGE MOTOR BIKE CLUB
P.O. Box 123
Carolina, RI 02812

or

JOHN F. MARTIN, PRESIDENT
VINTAGE MOTOR BIKE CLUB
P.O. Box 62
Montpelier, IN 47359

Old Pedal Cars

Elmer Duellman is an advanced collector. As usual he is always interested in buying, selling and trading to upgrade his fine collection.

You may contact him at:

Rt. 2 - Box 26
Fountain City, WI 54629

Wanted To Buy

Childrens Old Pedal Cars
Will buy any unrestored pre 1940's
also buy parts and sell cars

Randall Arterburn
Indianapolis, Indiana
1-317-631-5245

Buy – Sell – Trade

Pedal Cars • Large Steel Toys •
Buddy-L Keystone • Sturdy Toy Kingsbury, Etc.

Restoration Service on Pedal Cars and Pressed Steel Toys

DARWIN HUNKLER
2248 S. Cty., Rd. 350 W. • Russiaville, IN 46979
(317) 453-1210

Rusty Spokes

Al Rose
Vintage and Modern Bicycles

1711 W. 11th St
Upland, CA 91786   Ph (909) 985-0575

The Pedalers

Collectors of
Antique and Classic Bicycles

JAMES ALLEN & JAMIE ALLEN
Route 10, Box 935-48
Springfield, MO 65803
Phone: 417-833-1980

The Pedal Pusher

233 Penner Dr. • Pearl, MS 39208

Dedicated To The Balloon Tire Bicycles & Pedal Cars

PUBLISHED MONTHLY
To Arrive the 15th of Each Month

SUBSCRIPTIONS ARE $12.00 PER YEAR
Phone: (601) 932-6165
Fax: (601) 932-4490

1102 GREENE STREET, ADEL, IOWA 50003 • 515-993-5017

The Bike Shopper is published monthly by The Bike Shopper, Inc.

Send check or money order to:
$12.00 for 3rd class mail • $20.00 for 1st class mail

AMERICAN

Est. 1879   MAGAZINE

400 Skokie Blvd., Suite 395
Northbrook, IL 60062-7903

Place an ad with us!!

708-291-1117 or Fax: 708-559-4444

SEPTEMBER, 1932   19

Direct to You-30 Days' Trial

New Low Prices!
Write for
FREE Catalogue
and Our Big Offer

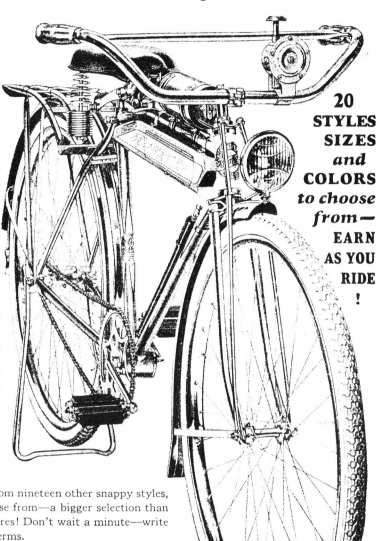

20 STYLES SIZES and COLORS to choose from— EARN AS YOU RIDE !

Now, boys, comes the biggest opportunity you've ever had to own this wonderful, genuine Ranger Bicycle. Our new low prices and special offers make it easy for you. And we'll let you ride it on 30 days' trial! The biggest thrill of your young life will be the day you get your Ranger.

What bicycles these are! Just take a look at the new features for 1932. Dazzling *chromium* front forks and mudguards; exquisitely graceful new auto style *chromium* lamp; Lobdell rims and all bright parts *chromium* plated; genuine grain leather saddle; patented light tubular rear carrier, rounded edge tool tank, famous Ranger smooth running sprocket and chain. The finest construction and equipment of any bicycle in the country—all improved free wheeling coaster brake models and fully guaranteed for five years.

It's just the bike for *you*. Ride for pleasure or profit. You can make money doing errands or delivery work for stores— and *make your Ranger pay for itself!*

Besides this Ranger, you may select from nineteen other snappy styles, colors and sizes. A great variety to choose from—a bigger selection than you'll find in most of the largest city stores! Don't wait a minute—write right now for our marvelous offers and terms.

Buy NOW Direct — Save Money!

Remember—this beautiful Ranger or any bike in our 1932 *free* catalogue is yours for 30 days' riding test. If you are not satisfied, return it at our expense.

To prove that our 1932 prices are down to rock bottom, we offer our new "Sentinel" Motorbike at the money-saving price of $18.85. Shown at the left.

$18 85 Cash

Send No Money!
Do not buy until you see our FREE 1932 illustrated catalogue. Describes many styles, sizes, colors. Lamps, wheels, equipment at *half* usual prices. Guaranteed tires from $1.50 up.

Buy from Bicycle Specialists and Save

We have been in business 40 years, and can offer you *greatest variety and lowest prices* for high grade bicycles.

Write today for FREE catalogue, and marvelous new low prices and terms

MEAD CYCLE CO. Dept. S-219, CHICAGO

12 So. Market St., near Madison St. Bridge

EDWARDS *Christmas*
SALE of 'ROADMASTERS'

$26⁹⁵

BOSTON COLLEGE VS. HOLY CROSS

DOUBLE SPRING
TROXEL
SADDLE

CLASS
REFLECTOR

NEW DEPARTURE
COASTER BRAKE

TORRINGTON BALL
BEARING PEDALS

Pay Only a Small Amount
Down on Our Convenient
Lay-Away or Budget
Plans to Buy That
"Roadmaster" Bicycle
to Make Your
Youngster Happy
This Christmas!

Full size bikes for
boys and girls — all
heavily constructed,
streamlined and sub-
stantially made with
such famous features
as Morrow Brake,
Troxel Saddle and
Heavy Balloon Tires!

★ Edwards—Sporting
Goods—Street Floor

THANKSGIVING DAY GAME!
Syracuse All-Star Scholastic Team
vs.
Manlius Cadets

No Charge for 2 Hours Parking with a Purchase of $1 or More at Edwards

The Ritz-Carlton Hotel on Atlantic City's famed boardwalk offers a bicycle checking and rental service to guests. Cycling is permitted on the boardwalk at certain hour and the sport may also be enjoyed on close-off streets nearby.

ALL AMERICAN MADE
LIGHTWEIGHT BICYCLE

The Manton & Smith Company, Chicago, Ill.,
recently introduced a line of made-in-America
lightweight bicycles. The model shown here
features full racing equipment, including track
racing tires, rims, saddle, handle bars and
pedals. The diamond frame model is ex-
tremely low built, with 2¾ inch sprocket drop
and 40-inch wheelbase. The new Manton &
Smith lightweights were designed by J. S.
"Jimmie" Manton, former racing cyclist, to
serve as all-purpose bicycles, although they
weigh only about one-half as much as a fully
equipped standard bicycle.

16

FOR WELL-ROUNDED CHRISTMAS STOCKS

● The fine reception given the Mercury De Luxe models earns them a place in every well-rounded Christmas stock. They are tops in "de luxe" and surprisingly moderate in price. We feel that they are the most beautiful bicycles in production.

Their "eye appeal" has been tested on hundreds of sales floors in competition with virtually every other make and the

results have been very gratifying to us and very profitable to the merchants.

These fully equipped models are styled to sell themselves and priced to compete in the volume market. If you have not already included them in your Christmas stock, by all means let us send you complete catalog and prices at once.

●

THE MURRAY OHIO MFG. COMPANY
CLEVELAND, OHIO

MERCURY

1940 Ad

"Westfield" Adult Bicycles

Clock & Speedometer Instrument Panel

List Prices Subject to Catalog Discount—See Page 1

Priced F.O.B. Westfield, Mass.

In keeping with a policy producing the very highest quality Bicycles at attractive prices, this 1940 "WESTFIELD" line introduces models which in construction, design, equipment and finish are the finest ever produced in the "COLUMBIA" Factory. All have NEW DEPARTURE Coaster Brakes; all fitted with Double Tube Balloon Tires except the Sport Models. Automobile Type Rear Reflectors, Chrome Rims and all bright parts Chromium Plated.

T396—Equipped Tank Model—$72.50

Streamline 18" Frame; Tank having Lock and Key. Chromium Plated Combination Horn-Lite. INSTRUMENT PANEL consisting of Clock and Speedometer. Streamline Saddle, Rear Luggage Carrier, Chain Guard and Pedals. Kick-up stand. Chrome Truss Rods, "Pope" Texas Handlebar, with cross-brace. Gothic Guards. Specify **RED or BLUE** Finish. *Priced F. O. B. Westfield, Massachusetts.*

"WESTFIELD" Light Weight Models

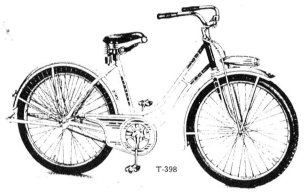

T398—Streamlined Woman's Model - - - - (As Illustrated)—$57.50

A beautiful Streamline model, with all the appointments desired in a high grade bicycle. Attractive TRI-COLOR trim. Full Metal Skirt Guard Lacing. Streamline Chain Guard, Chrome Truss Rods, Chrome Plated Reflecto-Lite. Electric Horn Tank (not illustrated), Gothic Guards, Rear Reflector. Parking Stand. New Departure Coaster Brake. Balloon Tires, etc. Frame 18" or 20". Specify Red or Blue Finish and Frame size desired.

T376—Woman's Model with Combination Horn-Lite—$56.30

Similar to Model T398 except FRAME. HEAD, in TWO COLOR COMBINATION. DOES NOT HAVE TRUSS RODS. Has SEMI-SKIRT METAL LACING. Frame 18" or 20". Specify Red or Blue Finish and Frame size desired.

T375—Streamline Women's Model—$51.70

Same as T376 EXCEPT WITHOUT COMBINATION HORN-LITE. Frame 18" or 20". Specify Red or Blue Finish and size desired.

T491—Men's Sports Roadster—$51.30

Special. Lightweight Model. Sports design fenders, front fender with tapered extension. Enameled Forged Crown Fork. Semi-Chain Guard. Tires; 26" x 1¼," U. S. Royal Master, double tube. Lightweight Rims. Rear Reflector. Hammock Spring Top Saddle. Frame 21". Specify **Azure Blue,** or **Carmine** color, with gold striping. All bright parts Chrome plated. NEW DEPARTURE Coaster Brake.

T492—Women's Sports Roadster—$51.30

Special Lightweight Model. Sports design fenders, front fender with tapered extension. Enameled Forged Crown Fork. Enameled Semi-Chain Guard. Tires; 26" x 1¼, U. S. Royal Master, double tube. Lightweight rims. Rear Reflector. Hammock Spring Top Saddle. Frame 20". Specify **Azure Blue,** or **Carmine** color with gold striping. All bright parts chrome plated. NEW DEPARTURE Coaster Brake.

Left—**T373**
Men's Streamline Motobike Fully Equipped—$57.80
FULL SIZE

Streamline Frame and Tank with Lock and Key. Electric Horn in Tank and Sound Louvres. Chrome Truss Rods. Streamline Rear Luggage Carrier, Parking Stand. Reflector. Delta Torpedo Light. Gothic Guards. "Pope" Texas Handlebar with cross-brace. Double Spring Saddle. New Departure Brake. Fine Balloon tires 26" x 2⅛". Frame 18" or 20". Specify Red or Blue Finish and Size Frame Desired.

Page 450   New York   BENNETT BROTHERS, Inc.   Chicago

18

1940 Ad

SILVER KING *Nationally Advertised* BICYCLES

Advertisements in Five Leading Magazines for Youngsters Create an Exclusive Market

Silver King's modern beauty, its strength and swiftness and lightness is making it a winner. The amazing progress of Silver King in the last few years is being added to by advertising in five leading magazines for youngsters. Once bicyclists are sold by this advertising, a market is created which only Silver King can satisfy. These are the features that are making the gleaming Silver King an outstanding favorite.

★ **Free Insurance**—only Silver King gives this complete protection without extra cost. Every Silver King is shipped with a policy attached which provides protection against fire and theft. (Rocket models not insured.)

★ **Spring Action Front Fork**—The positive spring action takes up the jarring shocks that come up the handlebars in ordinary bicycles. Available on all models shown here, except GT494.

★ **Longer Wheelbase**—As on automobiles, a longer wheelbase gives easier riding quality. Silver Kings have a wheelbase 1½ inches longer than any other bicycle.

★ **Stronger Frame**—Made of heat-treated aluminum alloy, the metal used in building modern trains and airliners. A pull of ten thousand pounds cannot separate the joints.

★ **Retractable Parking Stand**—A gentle forward push when the bicycle is started, and the parking stand springs up out of the way. A flick of the foot, and it's firmly in parking position.

★ **Complete Electrical Equipment**—Headlight, horn, and tail light are completely electrical, and are especially designed. Wiring connections are concealed wherever possible.

All Except Rockets INSURED FOR ONE YEAR AT NO EXTRA COST!

Silver King Rocket Bicycle with Motorbike Frame
GT497—$48.60

A boys' bicycle with all sorts of de luxe, built-in equipment that is usually found only at much higher prices. Check these remarkable features:

● Welded motorbike type frame with reinforced joints.
● Patented spring-action front fork that absorbs all the shocks that usually come through the handlebars on a bicycle.
● Finish of hand-rubbed baked enamel in brilliant, lasting colors, over a baked non-rusting prime coat.
● Colors: Red, blue, or black, trimmed with white. Black trimmed with red.
● Large twin electric headlights mounted on head.
● Streamlined tail with built-in electric horn.
● 26x2.125 double tube whitewall balloon tires.
● Streamlined chain guard. Padded saddle with double truss springs.
● Luggage carrier with built-in electric tail light.
● Wide chrome-plated handlebars. Regular type parking stand.
● Shipping weight, 70 lbs.

GT498—Girls' Silver King Rocket—$48.60
Made with the same specifications as GT497, except that it has drop-centre type frame and skirt lacing over the rear wheel.

Priced F.O.B. Chicago	*This Applies to the Bicycles Illustrated on This Page*

A Silver Beauty for Women, Light-Weight and Safer

GT494—$66.90

(Mfrs. Suggested Retail Price $89.95)

This strong, beautiful bicycle has a 19½" drop-centre frame, brilliantly polished. 24-inch wheels bring it closer to the ground, making it unusually safe. It comes equipped with combination electric horn and headlight, electric tail light, double tube whitewall balloon tires, retractable parking stand, chrome chain guard, and comfortable padded saddle. Shipping weight 67 lb. Price includes PREPAID INSURANCE.

The Favorite Silver King with Even More New Features
GT493—$66.90

(Mfrs. Suggested Retail Price $89.95)

More than twenty-five years' experience in bicycle engineering is back of this great Silver King. Its structural soundness, its silver brilliance and graceful streamlining make it truly the bicycle of tomorrow. Check these features:

● A frame three times as strong as steel. ● Bright all-silver finish, with aluminum parts buffed and steel chrome-plated. ● Front fork with patented spring action. ● 26-inch wheels, chrome-plated, with non-rusting spokes. ● Double tube 26x2.125 balloon tires with white sidewalls. ● Guards of stainless steel. ● Retractable parking stand, built on. ● Chain guard in chrome-plated wing design. ● Special saddle with double-truss, chrome-plated springs. Can be raised 4 to 5 inches. ● Diamond anti-friction twin roller chain ½-inch pitch by ⅛-inch. ● Combination Hornlite of exclusive design. ● Streamlined tail light. ● Coaster Brake, Morrow, Musselman, or New Departure. ● Net weight 48 lbs. ● Shipping weight 70½ lbs. ● PREPAID INSURANCE for one year.

MONARK SUPER FRAME BICYCLES

★ Insurance for 1 Year against fire and theft, at no extra cost.
★ New continuous double bar, safer "Super" frame.
★ Exclusive design retractable parking stand.
★ Patented spring action front fork which absorbs road shocks.

Men's Fully Equipped Tank Model Monark Bicycle
GT495—$54.40

(Mfrs. Suggested Retail Price $72.45)

A distinctive, fully equipped Bicycle with every safety feature. Built with stronger continuous bar, SUPER frame, and easy-riding, patented spring action front fork. Equipment includes twin headlights with individual switch controls; electric tail light built into luggage carrier; retractable parking stand; built-in horn; patented cushion front fork; and all the other exclusive Monark features. Finished in brilliant baked enamel. Shipping weight 70 lb. PREPAID INSURANCE at no extra cost. Red, Blue, or Black, trimmed with White.

Left
Women's Fully Equipped Touring Model Monark Bicycle
GT496—$54.40

(Mfrs. Suggested Retail Price $72.45)

The riding ease, safety, and beauty of this superb Bicycle appeal to the most particular feminine rider. The patented spring-action front fork is especially wonderful for a woman, as it absorbs all the harsh shocks that usually come through the handlebars of a bicycle, and this makes steering much easier. These additional features are big selling points, too:

● Drop-centre, four-bar "Super" frame, stronger without excessive weight.
● Combination electric horn and headlight on front fender. Electric tail light.
● Luggage carrier. Retractable parking stand.
● Skirt lacing over rear wheel. Extra wide mudguards. Streamlined chain guard.
● Double tube 26x2.125 whitewall balloon tires.
● Baked enamel finish: Red, blue, or black trimmed with white; blue or black trimmed with red; cream trimmed with red.
● PREPAID INSURANCE.
● Shipping weight 65 lb.

New York   BENNETT BROTHERS, INC.   Chicago   Page 449

1940 Ad

"Westfield" Adult and Juvenile Bicycles

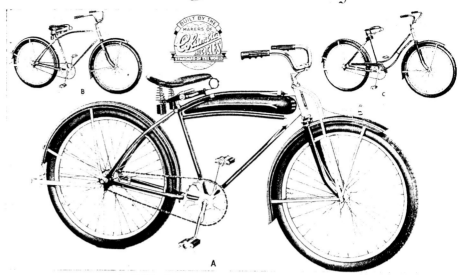

List Prices
Subject to Catalog
Discount—See Page 1

SPECIAL ATTENTION is called to these three low-priced Models. Each carries the "WESTFIELD" QUALITY standards of construction, but with a less expensive equipment. All have Double Tube Balloon Tires, NEW DEPARTURE Coaster Brakes, Parking Stands, comfortable Spring Saddles, Gothic type Fenders, and all bright parts Chrome plated. Specify RED or BLUE when ordering.

The Westfield Line is Priced F.O.B. Westfield, Massachusetts.

A—T473—Streamline Equipped Motobike—$50.40
(Full Size) Battery Tank and built-in Electric Horn. White Enamel Torpedo light and truss rods. Tires 26" x 2⅛".
B—T474—Roadster, Single Bar—$43.90
(Full Size) Tires 26" x 2⅛".
C—T475—Women's Bicycle—$45.40
(Full Size) Enameled Chain Guard. Tires 26" x 2⅛". Frame 18". Balloon tires. New Departure Brakes.

Columbia

"COLUMBIA" BALL-BEARING VELOCIPEDES

Superior construction, enameled in Carmine color with Ivory color head. Real bicycle Steel Frames. 1⅛" Chain Tread Solid Rubber Tires. Ball-bearing Wheels and Pedals. Adjustable Handlebar with Rubber Grips and Bell. Adjustable Saddle (streamlined) with Coil Springs and Ruby Reflector. Chrome Truss Rods.

Model	Ages	Wheels: Front	Rear	Price
T367	2-3 years	12½"	8"	$17.50
T368	3-4 years	16½"	10"	19.80
T369	4-5 years	20 "	14"	21.20
T370	5-7 years	24 "	16"	22.40

"WESTFIELD" BALL-BEARING VELOCIPEDES

Similar to "COLUMBIA" but have Enameled Forks, no Truss Rods, No Bell, smaller Guards and less expensive Handlebars, Stems, Saddles, etc. 1⅛" Solid Tires. Color—Blue—White Head and striping.

Model	Ages	Wheels: Front	Rear	Price
T487	2-3 years	12"	8"	$13.90
T488	3-4 years	16"	10"	16.10
T489	4-5 years	20"	14"	17.30
T490	5-7 years	24"	16"	18.40

Right   Girls' Unequipped Model

Here is a bicycle that will give great pleasure to the young girl. New Departure Coaster Brake. Reflector. Excellent Seat. Parking Stand. Exposed metal parts Chrome finished.

Model	Frame	Balloon Tires	Price
T406	15"	20" x 2⅛"	$43.50
T408	16"	24" x 2⅛"	46.30
T407	16½"	26" x 2⅛"	47.10

Specify RED or BLUE Finish

T-400

T400—Boys' Equipped Motobike—$53.60
(As Illustrated)
16½" Double bar frame with Built-in Tank, Rear Luggage Carrier, Truss Rods, "DELTA" Torpedo Lite, Gothic Guards, Double Tube Balloon Tires 26" x 2⅛". New Departure Coaster Brake. Parking Stand.

T401—Boys' Equipped Motobike—$52.60
Similar to above but SMALLER. Has 24" x 2⅛" Balloon Tires. 16" Frame.

T402—Boys' Unequipped Double Bar Frame Motobike—$47.80
Similar to above BUT WITHOUT TANK, LIGHT, LUGGAGE CARRIER. 16½" Double Bar Frame 26" x 2⅛" Balloon Tires.

Boys' Single Bar Frame Unequipped Models

Specify RED or BLUE Finish.

Model	Frame	Balloon Tires		Price
T404	15"	20" x 2⅛"	New Departure	$42.60
T405	16"	24" x 2⅛"	Coaster Brake	43.40
T403	16½"	26" x 2⅛"	Parking Stand	46.10

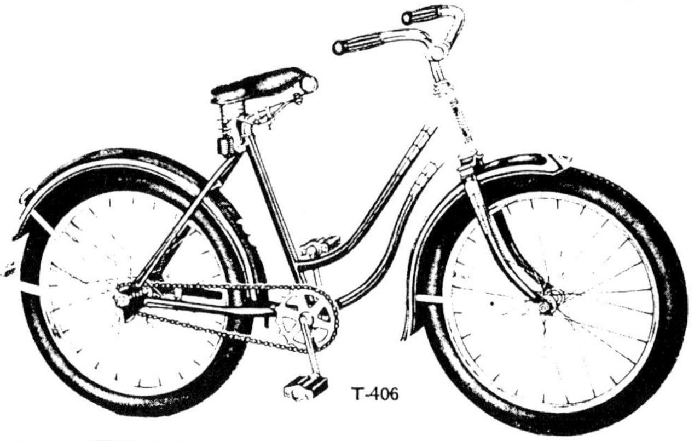

T-406

1941 Ads

Right—Anniversaries are good pegs on which to hang bicycle promotions. Charles "Mile-a-Minute" Murphy recently celebrated the 50th anniversary of his ride. Below—Bike Breakfast Run, for charity benefit, starting from Aug's in New York City.

Population 13,500; Bicycles 1,400

St. Augustine, Fla., With NATION'S Highest Per Capita of Cyclists, Shows Other Communities That They Have Room for Large Increases

Bicycles in one of the racks provided by the City of St. Augustine. This rack, which has a capacity of about 100, is in front of the Old Slave Market, opposite a movie theater.

HIBBARD, SPENCER, BARTLETT. & CO.

1497

AJAX BICYCLES.

Model 49, 28 in. wheels, · · · · · · · · · · · each $35.00

Frame.   Height, 21 or 23 in.; rear forks. 17⅛ in.; drop, 2½ in.
Head.   6⅞ in.
Tubing.   Shelby seamless steel; upright, top and lower tubes, 1⅛ in.; head, 1⅜ in.; bent D forks, ⅞ in., and D rear stays, ¾ in.
Connections.   Drop forged, flush throughout; seat post bolt screwing direct on seat post bushing; internal tapered reinforcements.
Forks.   Drop forged, oval diamond crown, finely nickel plated and polished; forks nickel plated at ends.
Wheel Base.   44½ in.
Wheels.   28 in.
Rims.   Fairbanks one-piece; stained mahogany, V-shaped.
Spokes.   Excelsior Needle Co's swaged; 15 × 17 gauge; 32 in front, 36 in rear; finely nickel plated.
Hubs.   New style barrel pattern; turned from solid bar.
Bearings.   Three point contact; cones turned from Sanderson's tool steel, tempered, ground and polished.
Balls. $\frac{3}{16}$ in. in front, ¼ in. in rear; $\frac{5}{16}$ in. in crank hanger; $\frac{3}{16}$ in. in head.
Cranks.   Fauber one-piece; oval; 6 or 6½ in. throw, finely nickel plated
Tread.   4⅞ in. (measured from outside of cranks).
Sprockets.   22-tooth front, 8 or 9-tooth rear.
Chain.   No. A Baldwin, $\frac{3}{16}$ in.
Guards.   Wood, stained mahogany to match rims, eyeletted, lacing cord color of frame.
Saddle.   Garford Brown pattern, No. 165.
Handle Bar.   19 in.; upturned Schinneer pattern 1⅜ in. stem.
Pedals.   H. & D. rubber.
Seat Post.   L front; nickel plated and polished.
Finish.   Three coats of enamel, dark royal blue or Brewster green, striped with red.
Accessories.   Oblong square tool bag, containing Springfield wrench, pump and oiler.
Tires.   M. & W. double tube.
Weight.   25 to 26 pounds, according to equipment.

Regular Equipment, 23 in. frame; 22 and 9-tooth sprockets (68⅔ gear); color blue; No. 165 Garford Brown pattern saddle; 19 in. upturned Schinneer pattern steel handle bar, M. & W. 1⅝ double tube tires; wood guards, stained mahogany to match rims, and lacing cord color of frame; H & D rubber combination pedals.

Options.   21 in. frame; color Brewster green; 8 tooth rear sprocket.
Where more expensive parts are ordered than those mentioned above, there will be an extra charge for the difference

The ELGIN Motor-Bike

Save $10.00 to $15

$32.45
EQUIPPED AS ILLUSTRATED

BUY AN ELGIN MOTOR-BIKE FOR REAL SATISFACTION

Note These Features:

Frame
Up to date motor-bike frame of approved truss type. Made of 1-inch seamless steel bicycle tubing, with thoroughly reinforced flush joints. Patterned after standard motorcycle frame design.

Size
Furnished in 22-inch size only, with dip in top frame bar, making it practical to raise or lower the seat post to permit comfortable riding for practically anyone who can ride a 20, 22 or 24-inch diamond frame bicycle.

Mud Guards and Stand
Mud guards are of drop side style, front guard fitted with rubber splasher and rear guard with stand lock clip. Substantial motor-bike type stand fastening to clip on rear mud guard when bicycle is being ridden.

The Elgin Motor-Bike Leads All Others
You Would Pay $40.00 to $45.00 Elsewhere for a Bicycle of This Quality

The latest ideas in up to date bicycle manufacturing combined with sturdy reliable construction make the Elgin Motor-Bike one of the finest bicycles on the market today. The remarkably fine finish of this bike is quickly recognized and universally appreciated. We are offering this wonderful bicycle at a price easily $10.00 to $15.00 lower than you are usually asked elsewhere for a bicycle of similar type.

NO BICYCLE POSSESSES MORE REAL FEATURES

Note These Features:

Saddle
High grade comfortable riding Troxel saddle of motor-bike type, with good grade leather top. Has beehive type cushion springs, black finish. Size of top, length over all, about 10¾ inches; width, about 8¼ inches.

Wheels and Rims
Steel rims, enameled to match the frame, crescent cement type, for 28-inch tires. Both front and rear wheels have 36 spokes. Front hub is spindle type; rear hub, New Departure Coaster Brake Hub.

Tool Equipment
Heavy leather tool bag, reinforced with black metal ends. Has nickel plated clasp and ring. Equipment includes telescope type bicycle pump, bicycle wrench, tube of tire repair cement and oiler.

Other Features of ELGIN Motor-Bike Model Leadership

Tires
The famous U. S. Rubber Company's Chain Tread Tires. 28x1½-inch size. (See page 454 for detailed description and illustration of these splendid tires.)

Handle Bars
Famous De Luxe Motor-Bike Bars of forward extension type. Complete with substantial reinforcing bar with diamond tapered ends. Up to date type Gripwell grips, about 5 inches long.

Front Fork
Approved motor-bike type.

Headlight Battery Container
Attractive tank between two top bars for storing headlight battery.

Pedals
Motor-bike type corrugated rubber pedals, with pedal rubbers removable or adjustable.

Chain
⅜x1-inch Diamond Roller Chain.

Hanger
One-piece drop forged crank with hanger lock ring.

Well designed sprocket, 26 teeth, of light weight. Has 7-inch tapering pedal crank.

Finish
An attractive cherry red with ivory head. Darts on bars and broad stripe down center of mud guard. Mud guards match frame finish.

The same finish is very widely used on many of the latest and best known makes of automobiles, being one of the best wearing finishes made. The many nickel plated metal parts complete a most attractive appearance.

28K1339¼—Our ELGIN Motor-Bike Model, equipped with New Departure Coaster Brake. Horn, Lamp and Luggage carrier, as illustrated. Shipping weight, 65 pounds.................................**$32.45**

28K1349¼—Our ELGIN Motor-Bike Model, equipped with New Departure Coaster Brake, but without horn, lamp or luggage carrier. Shipping weight, 65 pounds...................................**$29.95**

Three-cell flashlight batteries suitable for use with headlamp on 28K1339¼ bike, are shown on page 666 of this catalog.

Parcel Post, Express and Freight Rates Are on Pages 542 to 545

70 WHERE OHIO SAVES!
The Cussins & Fearn Co.,
22 Ohio Stores

WE'VE BUILT 'EM EVEN FINER

New Airflow Bike with Built-In Tank

$31.95

Our newest and most attractive 1937 model. Streamlined from front to back to keep pace with style trend of modern automobiles and trains. Streamlined light of tarnish proof chrome plated steel. All steel, drop center, chrome plated rims. Built for strength! Beautiful Airflow brilliantly enameled tank with handy light switch on top, battery clips inside. Large streamlined mud guards. Airflow design, chrome plated chain guard. Gleaming black enamel finish with red trim.

17T–4327—Airflow Bike with Tank **$31.95**

Buckeye Streamlined Bicycles for 1936

$28.95

Note the ruggedness of the double bar streamline frame! **Easier to pedal!** Strong fork reinforced by tubular chromium truss rods! **New type stainless steel mud guards!** Chrome rims! Large Genuine Leather Bucket Type Saddle! Chrome chain guard. Full streamlined Handle Bars. High grade Balloon Tires! Improved Famous Make Coaster Brake, positive action! Broad base parking stand. Red—Blue trim.

PAY C.&F. PENNY CLUB WAY
SEE PAGE 3

17T–4323 Buckeye Bicycle
$28.95

Our Biggest Value Streamlined Bicycle

$26.95

As Modern as the 1937 cars—and what a price! Full streamlined Double Bar Frame! **Big Balloon Tires!** Large Rubber Pedals! Extra heavy Broad Deep painted Mud Guards! **Famous Make Coaster Brake!** Motorcycle styled Handle Bars! Cherry red with black trim. Chrome Truss Rods and Rims. Buy on Easy Terms, only slightly higher.

17T–4322—Bicycle **$26.95**

Girl's Popular Model

Striking Beauty! Standard full size frame! Complete with Air-Flow enamel chain guard, parking stand, balloon tires, chrome rims, up to date designed handle bars, new streamline painted mud guards. Color, blue and white.

17T–4326 Girl's Bicycle
$23.95

A Quality Bike at a Low Price

with
Balloon Tires

There is no truer example of value than this Buckeye Bicycle! Durable and strong in construction. **Double Bar Frame,** large comfortable seat, extended mud guards over front wheel for beauty, large balloon tires, chrome finished rims. **Painted truss rods** add extra strength. High grade Famous Make Coaster Brake. Beautiful new cherry red and white trim finish.

17T–4321— Bicycle **$22.95**

(A) Auto Tone Horns
One stroke on the plunger produces a Double Signal—continued strokes produce practically an uninterrupted warning. It commands attention! Size 3x4 inches. Silverlac finish.
17T–4461—Horn ..59c

(B) Long Distance Siren
Gives a warning that compels attention. Brass outer drum highly nickel plated.
17T–4462—Siren ..89c

(C) French Type Bulb Horn
Looks like the attractive imported French Auto Horn. Has a pleasing, loud mellow tone. Clamps on the handle bar with clamp furnished. Soft rubber bulb. Nickeled horn. Nearly 9 inches long.
17T–4481—Horn ..19c

(D) Bike Bell
Nickel plated. Rotary movement. 1¾ inch gong.
17T–4464—Bell ..14c

(E) Bike Bell
Continuous ringing 2⅜ inch gong. Nicely finished.
17T–4463—Bell ..32c

(F) Electric Headlights
New, streamline design. Adjustable bracket to set light to best riding advantage. Complete with bulb. Battery case and cover strong and rigid. Carries one No. 6 dry cell battery —insulated to protect battery. Cover has lock prong. One piece bracket and switch in cap. Silverlac finish.
17T–4477 Headlight **$1.12**
15A–5489A ..14c
Dry cells extra, each..20c

(G) Ruby Reflectors
A warning signal for bicycles, motorcycles or autos. Attach to rear mud guard or license plate. Big ruby lens set in 1¼ inch aluminum setting with bolt for fastening. Shows strong red reflection when headlight rays from an auto in rear strike it.
17T–4478—Each....6c

(H) Tail Light
Attach to rear mudguard. Red lens and switch on top. Nickel finish. Uses 1 cell flashlight battery.
17T–4803—Each ..72c

(J) Flashlight Bracket
Adjustable to hold any flashlight. Nickel plated.
17T–4802—Each..30c

(K) Cyclometer
New Departure. Fits any 28 in. wheel. Registers up to 9,999 miles and repeats. Attached to front axle. Nickel plated.
17T–4471—Each, **$1.00**

(L) Handle Bar Basket
Made of corrugated hoop steel. Leather handle bar straps. Adjustable braces for holding basket level. Easily removed. Size 18x 13 in. 6 in. deep.
17T–4455. Basket, 96c

(M) Handle Bar Basket
Made of heavy tinned wire with reinforced steel braces. Adjustable lower brace so that basket carries level. Leather straps for handle bars and head. No scratching possible.
17T–4457 — 15x10x4¾ inch Basket.........62c

(N) Luggage Carrier
Made specially for bicycles of motor bike pattern, with extra long extension to reach in under saddle, to be attached to frame. Steel black enamel finish. Strong and substantial.
17T–4450. Carrier.29c

(O) Side Kickup Stand
Tempered spring steel with rubber tip. Frame brackets cadmium plated.
17T–4804—Stand..49c

(P) Stand
Raised or lowered with foot. Securely fastens to rear axle and locks securely in clip on rear mud guard when not in use. Made strong of channel iron and nicely enameled. Complete with mud guard clip.
17T–4400—Stand..29c

The "Belknap Special" Bicycle
...MEN'S...

Standard Belknap Equipment
—PLUS—
Delta Headlight
Delta Horn
Delta Tailight
Special Finish

An old favorite with new features at a price never before possible! 20 inch frame. 26x2⅛ inch Belknap Balloon Tires.

No. SBMB—Rich red enameled, white trim; chrome fittings; wt each 78 lbs _____ $78 00 Each

Crated.

Belknap DeLuxe Bicycles

Our Proudest Product ! !   DeLuxe Finish - - - DeLuxe Equipment - - - DeLuxe Design

Standard Belknap Equipment
— PLUS —
DeLuxe Delta Headlight
DeLuxe Delta Tailight
DeLuxe Tank
Electric Horn (in tank)
Chain Guard
Tubular Luggage Carrier
A "Rembrant" Paint Job !

Each

No. DBMB—Black enameled, white decorated.   20 in. frame; 26x2⅛ Belknap Balloon Tires_____ **$89 85**
Crated; wt each 85 lbs.

1939 Catalog Page

BEN HUR BICYCLES

Ben Hur Bicycles are made of one-inch tubing; spun heads; flush joints; reinforced at all connections; dust-proof construction at all bearing points. The bright and lustrous Polymerin finish is applied over a Bonderized base, previously sandblasted, producing a beautiful, hard and durable surface. Decorated with double arrow design; all bright parts are chromium plated.

MEN'S STANDARD WITH SPRING FORK

SPECIFICATIONS

Frame—Steel welded, double bar; with tank.

Fork—Knee action spring fork, with chromium plated truss rods.

Crank—One piece, 7 inch, offset; chromium plated.

Chain—$3/_{16}$x1 inch Diamond roller.

Fenders—Wide, crescent shape, enameled and striped to match.

Stand—Strong channel iron; attached to axle.

Sprockets—Fancy pattern; front 26 tooth, rear 10 tooth; chromium plated.

Wheels—26 inch; deep drop center rims; enameled finish.

Brake—New Departure coaster brake.

REGULAR EQUIPMENT

Tires—26x2⅛ double tube cord balloon.

Handle Bars—SB-26x8 inch; chromium finish, with rubber grips.

Saddle—Messenger sponge rubber.

Pedals—Large rubber padded.

Equipment—Large tank containing horn and battery tray; enameled self-contained fender light; luggage carrier; enameled chain guard and jeweled reflector.

Finish, Black with Cream Head and Trim

No. 97XES-18—18 inch frame . . . . Each $63.80

Approximate weight each, 64 lbs.; one in a carton.

CYCLE TRUCKS

DELIVERY BICYCLES

SPECIFICATIONS

Frame—Double bar, streamlined, counter braced, container brackets, cantilever construction.

Fork—Tubular type, drop forged.

Tires—Heavy duty; 20 in. front, 26 in. rear.

Rims—Extra heavy, chromium plated.

Handle Bar—Braced Boy Scout, 24 inch.

Finish—Enameled standard colors.

Stand—Wide, fork locking.

Sprockets—Front 22 tooth, rear 10 tooth.

Hubs—Front, motorcycle with ⅜ in. axle, ⅜ in. balls and $1^9/_{16}$ in. cup; rear, New Departure coaster.

Saddle—Messenger De Luxe.

Chain Guard—Chromium plated.

Basket—Extra strong with lid and hasp for padlock. Capacity—Will carry 150 lbs. easily.

★No. 38SCT—With 24x16x11 inch basket. . . . . .Each $78.00

★No. 38SCTL—With 28x22x11¼ inch basket. . . . . .Each 86.90

★No. 38SCTO—Without basket . . . . .Each 72.60

Weight each, 95 lbs.; one in a carton.

★*For shipment from factory at Chicago, Ill.*

27

1939 Catalog Page

BICYCLE SEAT POST BUSHINGS

Made of heavy metal, nickel plated finish, length 1⅜ inches, outside diameter ¹³/₁₆ inches; inside diameter ⅝ inches; fits No. 926 seat posts to any bicycle.

No. 925 ....Each **$0.20**
Weight each, 2 ozs.; packed loose.

BICYCLE HANDLE BARS

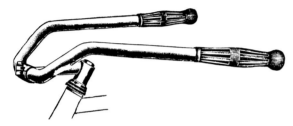

Without Grips or Stems

Made from ⅞ inch heavy gauge, seamless tubing; nickel plated on copper, highly polished; drop 3 inches; length of grip ends 12 inches; no forward bend.

No. 30SB—Width, 30 inches ....Each **$1.30**
No. 28SB—Width, 28 inches............Each **1.30**
Approximate weight each, 2 lbs.; packed loose.

BOY SCOUT

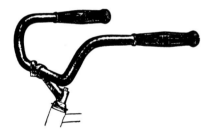

Without Grips or Stems

Made from ⅞ in. tubing; nickel plated on copper, highly polished; drop, 4 in.; no forward bend; width 20¾ in.

No. 130. Each **$1.30**
Wgt. each, 1¼ lbs.; packed loose.

BICYCLE HANDLE BAR GRIPS

ROLL FAST

Black Rubber
⅞ in. hole; 5½ inches long.

No. 108 ....Per Pair **$0.22**
Weight per pair, 8 ozs.; twelve pairs in a box.

Black Rubber
⅞ in. hole; 5½ in. long.

No. 115 ....Per Pair **$0.14**
Weight per pair, 8 ozs.; twelve pairs in a box.

BICYCLE HANDLE BAR GRIPS

Black Rubber
⅞ in. hole, 5½ inches long.

No. 107 ....Per Pair **$0.12**
Weight per pair, 8 ozs.; twelve pairs in a box.

Black Rubber
⅞ inch hole; 4½ in. long.

No. 126 ....Per Pair **$0.11**
Weight per pair, 4 oz.; twelve pairs in a box.

Black Rubber

⅝ inch hole, 3¼ inches long.

No. 131 ....Per Pair **$0.09**
Weight per pair, 1½ oz.; twelve pairs in a box.

¾ inch hole, 3¼ inches long.

No. 132 ....Per Pair **$0.09**
Weight per pair, 1¼ oz.; twelve pairs in a box.

½ inch hole, 3 inches long.

No. 143 ....Per Pair **$0.09**
Weight per pair, 1 oz.; twelve pairs in a box.

BICYCLE HANDLE BAR STEMS

WALD

Malleable steel, streamline design, heavily nickel plated, highly polished; 2¾ in. forward extension; adjustable hole for handle bar; expansion bolt and nut; ⅞x4 in. post.

No. 3 ....Each **$0.60**
Wgt. each, 1 lb.; ten in a box.

EXTENSION

Drop forged steel; 2¾ inch forward extension; adjustable hole for handle bar; expansion bolt and nut; ⅞x4½ inch post; nickel plated.

No. 25 ....Each **$0.60**
Weight each, ¾ lbs.; packed loose.

1939 Catalog Page

BICYCLE SPEEDOMETERS

STEWART-WARNER ROLLFAST

Tells How Far and How Fast

Aluminum finish case with chromium plated bezel; dial has brilliant red figures and markings on a grey background; streamlined pointer; head is 3⅛ inches wide and 2⅞ inches high; positive drive from sprocket secured to front wheel; attaches to handle bar and drive shaft follows truss rod to hub; complete with detailed installation instructions.

For Men's and Boy's Bicycles With Either 26 or 28 Inch Tires

No. 685CR ....Each *$4.45* 5.30

For Ladies' and Girls' Bicycles With Either 26 or 28 Inch Tires

No. 685DR ....Each *$4.45* 5.30
Weight each, 2 lbs.; one in an attractive box.

STEWART-WARNER ROLLFAST

With Separate Trip and Total Mileage Indicators

Beautiful crackle finished case, with chromium trim; shatter proof glass lens; has two mileage recorders—one for total miles traveled and another resets for each trip; fits bicycles with 28x1½ in. high pressure or 26x2.125 balloon tires; attaches to handle bar; furnished complete with necessary fittings and detailed installation instructions.

No. 785CR ....Each *$4.95* 5.90

Weight each, 2 lbs.; one in a box.

BICYCLE CYCLOMETERS

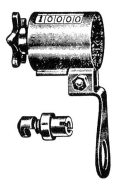

NEW DEPARTURE

An absolutely accurate instrument; records 10,000 miles and shows each tenth of a mile; figures are easily read from riders seat; highly polished nickel plated finish.

For 26 In. Balloon Type Tire Wheels

No. 26 ....Each $2.10
Wgt. each, 2½ oz.; one in a box.

BICYCLE MUD GUARD SPLASHERS

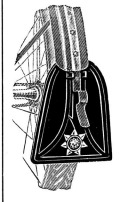

VELVET GRIP

Fits All Standard Mud Guards

Molded of rubber to a shape that fits the mud guard; a spring molded in the clamp gives a positive vise-like grip, holding the flap in correct position; may be used on either front or rear wheel; complete with jewel reflector mounted in chromium plated star and all necessary bolts.

No. 767 ....Each $0.40
Weight each, 4 oz.; packed loose.

BICYCLE STANDS

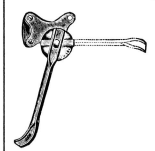

WALD

For 26 Inch Balloon Tired Bicycles

Rigid, strong and neat in appearance; always ready for instant use; easily and quickly operated by a slight kick; simple to attach, fastens to rear axle and clamps on lower rear fork; cadmium plated.

No. 67B ....Each $0.60
Weight each, 1¾ lbs.; packed loose.

CENTER KICK STAND

Consists of a cadmium plated steel rod to attach to frame as shown in illustration; strong coil spring holds the stand in either parking or riding position; changed instantly and easily from one position to the other with the foot.

No. 1001 ....Each $0.70
Weight each, 1¾ lbs.; packed loose.

BOLT-ON

Channel steel stand with heavy steel stamped clips which fasten on the rear axle and rest below the rear lower fork ends. A steel spring which holds the stand firm when not in use is included with bolts and nuts; satin steel finish.

For 26 Inch Balloon Tires

No. 63B-26 ....Each $0.55
Weight per carton, 19 lbs.; twelve stands in a carton.

BICYCLE STAND CLIPS

Suitable for bicycle stands; made of spring steel; rust-proof finish.

No. 1..............Each $0.10
Wgt. each, 1½ oz.; packed loose.

1939 Catalog Page

ELECTRIC BICYCLE LAMP AND GENERATOR SETS

DELTA

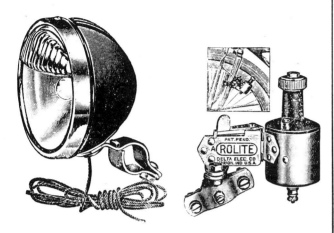

Lamp, black enameled steel with bright chrome rim; projects a bright piercing beam of light; mounts on handlebar of any bicycle; rust proof bracket; takes No. 31 Mazda bulb; bulb sockets are so designed that all generator bulbs are properly focused; unbreakable visor type lens.

Generator, precision built; 6 volts; operates from front tire; perfect alignment at all times; permanent magnetic rotor and stationary field coils; no moving contacts, brushes or slip rings to wear out; added pedal pressure less than 3 ounces; patented spring bracket so designed that tire wear is eliminated; cam lever for on-off position of the generator is easily controlled by hand while bicycle is in motion; lights at a walk, assuring adequate protection at all speeds.

Retail Price $4.95

No. A1876 . . . . .Each **$6.60**
Weight per set, 1¾ lbs.; one set in a box.

ELECTRIC BICYCLE LAMPS

DELTA PLASTILITE

Mounts on Handle Bar or Fender
Streamlined design; can be mounted on handlebar or front or rear fender; self-contained, using two standard 1¼ inch flashlight cells; unbreakable lens; case made of new molded plastic material, finished in white; length 8¼ inches; furnished complete but without batteries.

Retail Price $1.00

No. A1840 . . . . .Each **$1.45**
Weight each, ⅝ lb.; one in a box, twelve in a shipping carton.

ELECTRIC BICYCLE LAMPS

DELTA, NU-TORPEDO

Mounts on Handle Bar or Fender
Made of steel, finished in all white enamel; zinc plated bracket; by removing bracket the lamp may be mounted on the fender by drilling two ³/₁₆ inch holes; furnished with clear unbreakable lens; switch is automotive type and located so that lamp is waterproof; operates on two standard 1¼ inch flashlight cells, self-contained and No. 714 Mazda bulb; length 8¼ inches, diameter 2 inches; furnished complete but without batteries.

Retail Price $0.85

No. A1863 . . . . .Each **$0.85**
Weight each, ⅝ lb.; one in a box, twelve in a shiping carton.

DELTA SAFTYLITES

Mount on Front or Rear Axles
Polished aluminum bullet shaped twin cases; zinc plated brackets, rust and corrosion proof; plastic, non-breakable lens; one green light for the right side and one red light for the left side; a turn of the lens turns light on or off; easily installed on either front or rear wheel; uses No. 131 Mazda bulb; each light operates on one 1¼ in. flashlight cell; all self-contained, no wires; length 4 inches; complete but without batteries.

Retail Price Per Set (without batteries) $1.00

No. 1845 . . . . .Per Set **$1.45**
Weight per dozen sets, 7 lbs.; one set in a box, one dozen sets in a shipping carton.

DELTA REDBEAM TAIL LIGHT

Mounts on Rear Mudguard
Polished aluminum bullet shaped case; zinc plated bracket, rust-proof; plastic non-breakable red lens; a turn of the lens turns light on or off; easily installed on rear mudguard by drilling two ³/₁₆ in. holes; uses No. 131 Mazda bulb; operates on one 1¼ inch flashlight cell; all self-contained, no wires; length 4 inches; complete but without batteries.

Retail Price (without batteries) $0.50

No. 1846 . . . . .Each **$0.80**
Weight per dozen, 4 lbs.; one in a box, one dozen in a shipping carton.

Streamlined AIR-FLYTE Bikes at BARGAIN PRICES! Choice of Boys' or Girls'

...y your bike now, Pay-
...u-Ride, use C & F
...y Club Plan!
...r Beauty, Comfort and
...Riding, use an Air-
...!
...ied - to - the - minute in
...tiful Auto Color Com-
...tions!
...uipped with Torpedo
...light for Night Riding
...y!

If you want your boy or girl to have a fine Bicycle with smart 1941 appearance, and if you want
to Save Money, Buy this Modern, 1941 Streamlined
Air-Flyte Bicycle!

Guaranteed Double Bar Frame, Heavy Mud Guards
for Durability, Side Kick-up Stand. Big, Easy-
riding Balloon Tires with Heavy Tubes, smart look-
ing comfortable Saddle, New Departure Coaster
Brake. Girl's Model equipped with Chain Guard.

FEATURES

- Spring Saddle
- Crown Fenders
- Torpedo Headlight
- Kick-up Stand
- Balloon Tires Size 26x2.125
- Girls or Ladies Model has Chain Guard

2T-4056—Boy's Model, finished in maroon and
cream. Price $21.50
2T-4057—Girl's Model. Finished in blue and
cream. Price 21.50

$21.50 FULL SIZE

FISK BALLOON BIKE TIRES

...E AIR - FLIGHT. The indus-
...new and fine balloon. Two plies
...rong, resilient Fisk cord, with
...s famous Air-Flight tread.
...er style — greater value — better
...' qualities—longer mileage.

-4188—Black Side Size 26x2.125 in... **$1.69**
-4189—White Side Size 26x2.125 in..... **$1.89**

THE STANDARD. Also constructed of two plies of heavy
cord fabric, with the same rugged
tread and sidewall design as the
former Fisk Rugged Heavy Duty
tire. A leader in the economy
class.

17T-4190 — Black Side Walls.
Size 26x2.125
in. **$1.49**

Fisk Red Molded Balloon Tubes

This Fisk Inner Tube
for Balloon Bike Tires is
molded just like an auto
tube. Made of Red Rub-
ber and built to give long
service.

17T-4191—Tube for
26x2.125 inch
Bike Tires **72c**

FISK HI-PRESSURE BIKE TIRES

THE VICTOR is made of the popular construction: two plies with a
puncture resisting breaker strip. The
three plies under the tread give free-
dom from punctures, while retaining
the flexibility and easy riding qualities of the two-ply tire. The heavy
tread gives complete satisfaction in
uniform, durable wear.

17T-4192—White Side
Walls. Size 28 in........ **$1.39**

THE SKY-WAY is constructed
of two plies of fine quality fabric.
It is made with the same heavy,
laminated tube as is used in all Fisk
single tube bicycle tires. The tough,
black tread of the popular chain type
design is sure gripping and long
wearing.

17T-4194—White Side
Walls. Size 28 in........ **$1.25**

31

1961 Catalog Page

BICYCLES
—BLUE GRASS—DE LUXE—CHROME FINISH
BOY'S—26-INCH

Frame—Twin arch—all chrome.
Seat Post—Cadmium.
Chain Guard—Maroom with white decorations.
Tank—Chrome—red and gold decorations with Delta built-in double headlights and horn.
Horn—Delta—single cell—built in tank.
Luggage Carrier—Maroon de luxe with two reflectors.
Fork—All chrome.
Fenders—Gothic, chrome plated.
Headlight—Dual, chrome.
Reflector—Red glass, 1¾-inch.
Rims—Chrome.
Tires—26x1.75, Belknap white sidewalls.
Brake—Bendix.
Front Sprocket—48 Tooth, ½-inch pitch.
Rear Sprocket—19 tooth.
Chain—½-inch pitch.
Stem—Double adjusted. Chrome.
Grips—White rubber.
Kickstand—Cadmium plated.
Saddle—All white with chrome crash rail.
Pedals—Bow, black rubber.
Handlebar—Chrome.
Crank—Chrome, 26 inches.

D61-BG4_____ • __   Each
                            $159 45
One in shp ctn; wt each 56 lbs.

32

1961 Catalog Page

BICYCLES
—BLUE GRASS—

BOY'S

Frame—Twin arch, satellite red with white head.
Seat Post—Cadmium.
Chain Guard—Satellite red, ''Blue Grass'' in red on white stripe.
Tank—Satellite red, ''Blue Grass'' red with white decoration.
Luggage Carrier—Satellite red, with w h i t e decoration heavy duty.
Fork—Satellite red, white decoration. 3-plate crown.
Fenders—Deep crescent, satellite red, white tip front and white stripe.
Headlite—Chrome top.
Reflector—Red, 1¾-inch.
Rims—Enameled—white, red stripe.
Brake—Bendix.
Chain—½-inch pitch.
Stem—Double adjusted. Chrome plated.
Grips—White rubber.
Kickstand—Cadmium.
Saddle—De luxe, red and white.
Pedals—Black rubber.
Handlebar—Chrome plated, 24x6 inches.
Crank—Chrome.

GIRL'S

Frame—Twin arch, blue with white head.
Seat Post—Cadmium.
Chain Guard—Blue. ''Blue Grass'' in blue on white stripe.
Tank—Blue—girl's style. ''Blue Grass'' in blue with white decoration.
Luggage Carrier—Blue, with white decoration heavy duty.
Fork—Blue, white decoration. 3-plate crown.
Fenders—Deep crescent—blue, white tip front and white stripe.
Headlite—Chrome top.
Reflector—Red, 1¾-inch.
Rims—Enameled—white, red stripe.
Brake—Bendix.
Chain—½-inch pitch.
Stem—Double adjusted, chrome plated.
Grips—White rubber.
Kickstand—Cadmium.
Saddle—De luxe, blue and white.
Pedals—Black rubber.
Handlebar—Chrome plated, 24x6 inches.
Crank—Chrome.

26 INCH MODEL—26x1.75 BELKNAP TIRES

		Each
D61-BG64—Boy's model		$111 30
D61-BG65—Girl's model		

One in shp ctn; wt each 51 lbs.

24 INCH MODEL—24x1.75 BELKNAP TIRES

		Each
D61-BG44—Boy's model		$108 15
D61-BG45—Girl's model		

One in shp ctn; wt each 49 lbs.

1961 Catalog Page

BICYCLE LIGHTS
DELTA—ROADLIGHTER

Visor, retainer ring and reflector are all one piece. Snap-in lens; makes bulb changing a snap.

Adjustable head.

Heavy chrome-plated finish.

Clean flowing design, with "built-in" visor.

Stem mounting bracket.

Operates on 2 standard 1¼-inch flashlight cells.

Bulb: No. 14 or No. P-44016 Delta.

D62-A2815 _____Each **$4 88**
One in box; 12 in shp ctn; wt each 1 lb.   *$2 59*

DELTA ROCKET—RAY

Self-contained bicycle headlight with chrome visor. Positive on and off switch under lower shell for protection from weather.

Mounts easily and quickly on either handlebar or front fender. Operates on 2 Standard flashlight cells.

Takes bulb No. D96-14.

Batteries Not Included

White baked enamel finish with chrome finish.
D62-A2191 _____Each **$4 69**
One in box; 12 in shp ctn; wt each 1 lb.   *$2 49*

DELTA—Hi-Fin Single

For fender or handlebar mounting.

White finish with brite trim. Operates on two standard flashlight cells; uses D96-14 bulb.

Length 9 inches.

D62-A1747 _____Each **$3 72**
One in box; 12 in shp ctn; wt each ¾ lb.   *$1 98*

DELTA—Hawk

For fender or handlebar mounting.

White enamel lower; top shell chrome plated. Top operates on hinge.

Operates on two standard flashlight batteries; uses D96-14 bulb.

Length 8¼ inches.
D62-A2780C ___ _____Each **$3 56**
One in box; 12 in shp ctn; wt each ⅔ lb.   *$1 89*

BICYCLE LIGHTS
DELTA DE LUXE

White baked enamel finish. Amber jewel on lens, red jewel on top—both light up when headlight is lighted

Takes D96-14 bulb.

Operates on two standard flashlight cells. Length 8¼ inches.

D62-A2580—Complete less batteries __Each **$3 37**
One in box; 12 in shp ctn; wt each ⅔ lb.   *$1 79*

DELTA—STREAMLINE ELECTRIC
Steel body, white baked-on enamel with a bright trim. Unbreakable lens; zinc plated, rustproof brackets.

May be used on handle bar or fender.

Operates on two standard flashlight cells. Complete with Mazda bulb.

Batteries not included
Headlight; length 8¼ ins; diam 2¼ ins.
D62-A1880_____Each **$2 80**
One in box; wt each ½ lb.   *$1 49*

BICYCLE STOP LIGHTS

DELTA RED BEAM ELECTRIC

Tail Light

White plastic case and red plastic lens. Turn lens for light on or off. Mounts easily on rear mudguard of any bicycle. Operates from single, standard flashlight cell.

Battery Not Included
Tail light; length 4¾ ins; greatest diam 2 ins.
D62-A1846_____Each **$1 80**
One in box; 12 in shp ctn; wt ctn 3 lbs.   *$0 95*

BICYCLE HORNS

WALD
Chrome plated; single cell.
Attractive front grille, easily mounted on handle bar, efficiently operated by pressing button.
(Battery Not Included.)

D62-737 _____Each **$1 98**
10 in box; wt each ½ lb.

1961 Catalog Page

BICYCLE PEDALS
PERSONS—MEN'S

Precision machined from solid bar steel; heavy gauge steel tubing axle housing. All metal parts nickel plated; each pedal contains 10 ball bearings; high quality black rubber treads with non-slip deep grooves. ½ inch spindle will fit all models of American made bicycles.

Adult Size

D62-18 _ _ _ _ _ _ _ _ _ _ _ _ _ _ _   Pr $2 40

24 prs in shp ctn; wt pr 1½ lbs.

BICYCLE FLAPS
UNIVERSAL, With Red Reflector Jewels

Molded rubber, chrome ornaments with red reflector jewels.

Bolts fast to all mud guards, both front and rear. Two reinforced holes and bolts hold flap in proper position.

Height 10 inches.
Width 10½ inches.

BLACK
D62-84-A _ _ _ _ _ _ _ _ _ _ _ _ _ _ _ Each $1 89

WHITE
D62-84AW _ _ _ _ _ _ _ _ _ _ _ _ _ _ _ Each   2 40

One in poly bag; 48 in shp ctn; wt ctn 33 lbs.

TINGLEY

Heavy moulded rubber with racing flag design. Hole molded in the tip for fastening to bicycle fender.

D62-69W _ _ _ _ _ Each $1 35

One in poly bag; wt each 5 ozs.

Black rubber, with chrome ornament and jewel.

Height 7⅛ inches. Width 5¾ inches.

D62-76A _ _ _ _ _ _ _ _ _ _ _ _ _ Each $0 66

12 in box; wt doz 3 lbs.

BICYCLE MIRRORS
WALD

Pentagonally shaped flat mirror, with double-eye reflectors on back. Universal joint style rod.
Chrome plated.
Length—5½ inches.
Width—2¼ inches.

D62-74 _ _ _ _ _ _ Each $1 89

12 in box; wt box 6 lbs.

BICYCLE MIRRORS

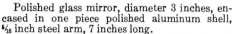

WALD

Round, flat mirror, chrome plated with single reflector on back, with Universal joint style rod. Diameter 3⅝ inches.

D62-72 _ _ _ _ _ _ _ _ _ _ _ _ _ _ Each $1 59

24 in box; wt box 9½ lbs.

WALD—REAR VIEW MIRROR

Polished glass mirror, diameter 3 inches, encased in one piece polished aluminum shell, ⁵⁄₁₆ inch steel arm, 7 inches long.

Arm attached to mirror case with ball and socket joint. Mirror can be set at any desired position.

Bracket clamp fits rigidly to handle bar top. Arms and clamps are satin plated finish.

D62-78 _ _ _ _ _ _ _ _ _ _ _ _ _ _ Each $0 90

24 in box; wt box 9½ lbs.

BICYCLE REFLECTORS

Red glass reflector for mounting on rear mud guard.

	D62-127	D62-1126
Diam reflector, ins	2⅛	3¼
Wt doz, lbs _ _ _ _ _	7	9½
Each _ _ _ _ _ _ _ _ _	$0 33	75

12 in box.

Red glass Diamond cut silvered on back. Especially constructed to attach to mud guard or rear axle.

D62-21—Diam glass 1 in _ _ _ Each $0 18

Loose; wt doz 1 lb.

BICYCLE LIGHTS
DELTA—Hi-Fin Twin

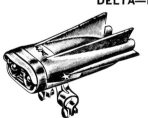

For fender or handlebar mounting.

White finish with brite trim.

Operates on four standard flashlight cells; uses two D96-14 bulbs.

Length 9 inches.

D62-A1744 _ Each $6 58

One in box; 12 in shp ctn; wt each 1¼ lbs.   *$3 49*

1961 Catalog Page

BICYCLE HORNS

Quality-made. Two-tone. Designed in automotive manner — Large sizing to compel consumer attention and add smartness to vehicles to which they are fitted.

Made with sturdy, swivel bracket for directional adjustments. Fit all standard bicycle handlebars. Easily attached. All working parts are replaceable. Beautifully plated and polished. Carefully tested. Fits all standard handlebars.

D62-105 Length 11¾ in._____ Each **$4 80**
50 in shp ctn; wt each 14 ozs.

HOLLYWOOD GOOSE HORN

Gives a honking sound in loud, resonant tones. Black live-rubber bulb. Nickel brass ferrule clamp designed to fit in protected position in crotch of handle bars. Fits securely to the front of handle bar near the steering post. Overall length 9 inches with a 2½ inch flared bell.

Silver gray, hammertone finish.
D62-400 _____ Each **$2 10**

Chrome plated.
D62-425 _____ Each **2 97**
One in box; wt each 6 ozs.

YODER DUAL TONE

Bell of horn is one piece die cast, zinc alloy finished
Bulb of moulded black rubber, dual tone voice. Rustproof and aluminum reed.
Overall length 9¼ inches, diameter of flared bell 2⅛ inches.

D62-420_____ Each **$2 04**
One in box; wt each 7 ozs.

BICYCLE SIREN
PERSONS BALLOON SIREN
Streamlined.

Nickel plated.
Designed for attaching to side of front fork, operating directly against side of tire, giving a loud shrilling sound.
Complete with clamp, bolts, nuts and 20 inch chain.
Diameter case 8 inches.
D62-150
Each **$4 73**
One in box; wt each 1¼ lbs.

SIRENS
PERSONS—JUNIOR WILDCAT

Ideal for tricycles, bicycles and pedal cars. Hand-crank operated, fool-proof mechanism. No batteries required.
Strong steel, beautiful chrome plated housing. Teardrop shape. Bracket fits any size handlebar. Makes sound like regular police siren.
Diameter 2½ inches; length 3½ inches.

D62-200_____ Each **$3 45**
One in box; wt each 8 ozs.

BICYCLE BELLS

DOUBLE CHIME

Nickel plated and polished, decorated with wheel design; rotary lever movement; adjustable handle bar clamp.
Diameter bell 2¼ inches.

D62-X71R
Each **$1 05**
One doz in box; wt doz 4 lbs.

Wrought metal, nickel plated with black base and handle bar clamp.
Adjustable handle bar clamp.
Diameter 2 inches.

D62X18R
Each **$0 90**
One doz in box; wt doz 2 lbs.

BICYCLE SPEEDOMETERS
ROLL FAST
Registers Speed and Distance.

Newly designed. Non-breakable lens; rugged two-position bracket; conventional handle bar mounting; one-piece noiseless drive gear.
Smart, easily read face dial; sweep-action mileage pointer; sturdy, shockproof, non-rust case.
Has two Odometers, one registers speed, the other mileage. Mileage reset, and trip mileage up to 10 miles in tenths.
Diameter 2¹¹⁄₁₆ inches; depth 1⁴⁷⁄₆₄ inches.

D62-753S_____ Each **$13 35**
One in box; 20 in shp ctn; wt each 1½ lbs.

1962 Catalog Page

APACHE DELUXE SPORTS BIKE

A Columbia sports bike of superb styling and finish—now in improved dress and equipment! Three Speed Coaster Brake. Columbia Twinbar Cantilever frame. Front and rear Chrome Carriers with spring luggage retainers. Stem-mounted battery-contained chrome Headlight. Columbia lightweight "Swept-Wing" Chain Guard. New two-tone Saddle with Crash Rail and all chrome hardware. White sidewall Tires. Chrome Airline Fenders. Chrome Fork Crown Cap. New Columbia plastic Grips matching frame color. Columbia built-in Kickstand. 1-3/4" White Side-Wall Tires.

No. 5625—26" Boys—Flamobyant Blue —   **117.60**

FIRE-ARROW SPORTS BIKE

NEW Cantilever Frame — NEW Columbia Aero-Tank with Twin Headlights and Horn — NEW Columbia front and rear Spring Top Carriers in chrome with truss-rod-bumper effect. Front carrier attached to fork — NEW Columbia-Name plastic Grips with flattened top — NEW Gold Mylar Trim on top tube and chain guard — NEW Two-Tone Saddle with Crash Rail and chrome hardware — NEW Bow Pedals with reflector jewels. — Chrome Airline Fenders. Regular Coaster Brake. Chrome Fork Cap. Exclusive Columbia Built-In Kickstand. Easy-Roll 1.75" Medium Pressure White Side Wall Tires. Patented Columbia Automatic Chain Oiler and Cleaner.

No. 5622—26" Boys—Flamboyant Red —   **103.20**

SLIM LINE BIKE
COLUMBIA

"THUNDERBOLT"

New features in these deluxe new fully equipped bikes! Girl's Twinbar. New Slimline Tank with Electric Horn. New front Guard-Rods with plate-mounted Twin Chrome Headlights. New tubular Slimline Rear Carrier with flat decorated top. Two-Tone lightweight saddle. Exclusive Columbia Airline Fenders and Swept-Wing Chain Guard. White Sidewall 1-3/4" American-made Tires. Flamboyant Turquoise enamel finish.

No. 4627—26" Girls, flamboyant turquoise.   **81.00**

THUNDERBOLT "SLIMLINE" BIKE

A new restyled series bike fully equipped with Twin bar cantilever frame, new Slimline tank with electric horn. New front Guard Rods with plated mounted twin chrome headlights. New tubular slimline rear carrier with flat decorated top. Two-tone lightweight saddle. Exclusive airline fenders and swept-wing chain guard. White sidewall 1¾" American made tires. Columbia Lubri-Kleen chain oiler and cleaner. Flamboyant enamel finish.

No. 3627—26" Boys—Flamboyant Red —   81.00
No. 3427—24" Boys—Flamboyant Red —   79.00

Article in the December 1993 Issue of
The Pedal Pusher

TWAS THE NIGHT BEFORE CHRISTMAS IN ELFLAND
AND SANTA DIDN'T KNOW WHAT TO DO
ALL HIS REINDEER (INCLUDING RUDOLPH)
HAD COME DOWN WITH REINDEER FLU

HIS SLEIGH WAS ALL PACKED AND READY
BUT HIS WORK WAS NOT YET DONE
THEN AN IDEA HIT HIM
HE PICKED UP THE PHONE AND DIALED 911

HE HAD TO MAKE HIS DELIVERIES
AS NOT TO DISAPPOINT ALL THE LITTLE TYKES
THEN TO HIS AMAZEMENT AND RESCUE
CAME THE PEOPLE WITH THE COLLECTOR BIKES

THE SIGHT THEY MADE IN THE MIDNIGHT SKY
LEFT SOME A LITTLE PERPLEXED
BICYCLES PULLING A SLEIGH ???
WHAT WILL THEY THINK OF NEXT ???

THINGS HAD WORKED OUT OKAY
SANTA GRINNED FROM EAR TO EAR
A MERRY CHRISTMAS TO ALL
    ... AND A HAPPY NEW YEAR!

ON SHELBY ~ ON HIGGINS ~ ON ROLLFAST
ON WESTERN FLYER ~ ON SCHWINN ~
ON COLUMBIA ~ ON ROADMASTER ~
ON HAWTHORNE
RIGHT TURN ELGIN, WHO DO YOU THINK
YOU ARE ?? ~ RUDOLPH ?

WRITTEN BY
LONGFELLOW ALLEN
ILLUSTRATED BY
PICASSO FRISING ---

Photographs

This is Bob Holder, age 13, taken in 1940 with his Bluebird Elgin.
(Bob is the father of collector Kerry Holder)

Pictured with some of his collection is Kerry Holder.
(1880's Columbia • 1880's Gurmley Jefferies • 1880's Rudge • 1880's Columbia)

Trading Card

Keat Bugle

Hub Lamps

Bells

Columbia Bicycles & Tricycles The Pope Mfg., Co.

Photographs

1935 Aero Cycle
with original owner, Bob Nichols.

40

Sheet Music

A BICYCLE Built For TWO

(ALSO KNOWN AS "DAISY BELL")

Words and Music by HARRY DACRE

with
UKELELE CHORDS
GUITAR CHORDS
and
SPECIAL HAWAIIAN
GUITAR CHORUS

EDDIE DUCHIN
and His Central Park Casino Orchestra

From a 1967 Schwinn Catalog

Schwinn HEAVY-DUTI®

Schwinn **DELIVERY BIKES**

The "dependables" from Schwinn.

When there's work to be done these durable delivery bikes fill the bill.

The ideal choice for quick, efficient, low-cost delivery service.

Schwinn CYCLE TRUCK®

Schwinn JUNIOR STING-RAY®   Schwinn LIL' CHIK™   Schwinn MIDGET STIN

From a 1967 Schwinn Catalog

24-INCH JUNIOR BIKES FOR GIRLS 7 TO 9 YEARS OLD

Schwinn DELUXE BREEZE®   *Schwinn* BREEZE®   *Schwinn* FIESTA®

26-INCH MIDDLEWEIGHT BIKES FOR GIRLS

Schwinn DELUXE HOLLYWOOD®   *Schwinn* STARLET® III   *Schwinn* HOLLYWOOD®

From a 1964 Schwinn Catalog

Middleweight Bikes for Boys
with 1 ¾-inch wide tires

Schwinn **MARK V JAGUAR**   Schwinn **CORVETTE**

Juvenile bikes . . . what a wonderful idea for a growing family! These Schwinn models are designed for the young boy or girl in your family. The top bars on Bantam and Pixie are removable to convert from boys' to girls' models.

Schwinn **BANTAM**   Schwinn **PIXIE**

From a 1964 Schwinn Catalog

𝒮𝒸𝒽𝓌𝒾𝓃𝓃 **DELIVERY BIKES** . . . ideal for

low-priced, economical delivery service for drug stores,

delicatessens, markets, news agencies and others. Specially

made with extra strength frames and heavy duty equipment.

𝒮𝒸𝒽𝓌𝒾𝓃𝓃 **WASP**   𝒮𝒸𝒽𝓌𝒾𝓃𝓃 **CYCLE TRUCK**

𝒮𝒸𝒽𝓌𝒾𝓃𝓃 **Deluxe AMERICAN**   𝒮𝒸𝒽𝓌𝒾𝓃𝓃 **AMERICAN**

Postcards

Cartoon Postcard
Mike Riach

Ocean City New Jersey Postcard
Mike Riach

Postcards

1950's Postcard of a Columbia Bike Store
Mike Riach

1968 Postcard of a Schwinn Bike Store
Mike Riach

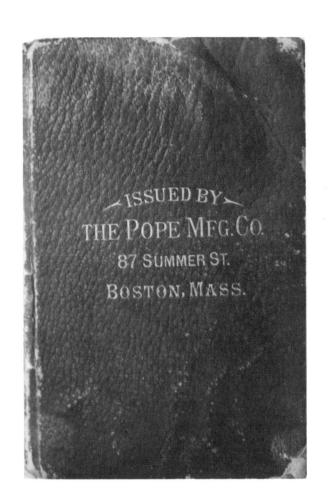

This book Published by the Pope Mfg., Co.
April 1880, in Boston, Mass.
Al Rose

A Columbia 1880 "Uncle Ike"
on back of Photo dated 1880.
Al Rose

Late 1950's AMF Roadmaster
Texas Rangerette - Original
26" Middle Weight
Dan Lepro

1960's AMF Royal Master
Jeff Meyers

1950's B.F. Goodrich
w/red light & siren
Jerrell Little

1960's B.F. Goodrich
Challenger - 26" Original
Mike Riach

1960's B.F. Goodrich Challenger
26" Original
Mike Riach

Colson - Evans
Bought from original owner
Jerrell Little

1920's Colson "Fairy" Tricycle
Original
Meghan Lauer

1930's Colson Tandem - Ladies ride in front &
Gentlemen steer from the back.
Jim Hoss

1935 Colson Flyer - Original
26" Balloon
Dan Lepro

1935 Colson Aristocrat
Original
Steve Castelli

1936 Colson
Original
Steve Castelli

1937 Colson Commander
Original
Steve Castelli

1939 Colson-Firestone "Super Cruiser"
Restored
Alan Kinsey

1939 Colson-Goodyear
"Clipper"
Original
Alan Kinsey

1939 Colson Imperial
Original
Steve Castelli

1939-41 Colson Tandem,
model 2610, rear steering.
Original (except tires)
Bob Harton

1940 Colson Twin Cushion
Steve Castelli

1940 Colson
Original
Hugh Rosenweig

1941 Colson, Ladies Clipper
James & Jamie Allen

1950's Colson-Evans
26", Spring Front
Romeo Ghamo

1954 Colson Cadet
20", Original
Gary DeDontney

1957 Colson-Evans
24", Original
Nic Frising
The Old Bicycle Shoppe

1960's Colson-Evans
24"
Brad Guilford

1885 Columbia Expert, 52"
This bike set the world record from
San Francisco to Boston, 3428 miles
in 33 days & 7 hours in 1992.
Steve Carter

1886 Columbia Light Roadster, 55"
Ty Cutkomp

1888 Columbia Light Roadster, 55"
Original, missing brake hardware
Peggy Mueller

1889 Columbia Tandem Tricycle
Steve Carter

1891 Columbia Light Roadster
53", Full Nickel, has won
Wheelmen Senior Award
Steve Carter

1893 Columbia Expert Ordinary, 50"
1917 Utica Cycle Co. w/wooden rims, 28"
John T. Dizer & William D. Dizer

1895 Columbia
Original
Hugh Rosensweig

1910 Columbia Springer
Shaft Drive
Steve Castelli

1933-34 Columbia Motobike
26" wheels,
2 speed new departure
Jim Agan

1937 Columbia Air-Rider
Steve Castelli

1938 Columbia Twin Bar
Donald Vaughn

1939 Columbia
Original
Alan Kinsey

1940 Columbia Superb
Original
Larry Helfand

1940 Columbia
Original
Steve Castelli

1941 Columbia Superb F9T
Chuck Cook

1943 Columbia - U.S. Army
Original tool pouch & tools also has
wooden pedals.
Jerrell Little

1942 Columbia
Original
Elery L. Beale

1948 Columbia
Restored
Gary DeDontney

1950 Columbia 5-Star Superb
Original
Larry Helfand

1951 Columbia 5-Star Deluxe
Donald Vaughn

1951 Columbia 5-Star
Original
Larry Helfand

1951 Columbia 5-Star Supreme
Original
Larry Helfand

1951 Columbia 5-Star
Original
Don W. Jensen

1952 Columbia w/Racycle Nameplate
Original
Craig Gray

1953 Columbia 5-Star
Original
Don W. Jensen

1954 Columbia 5-Star Super
26"
Sherm Rhymers

1954 Columbia
Original
Bob Nichols

1959 Columbia
26" Girls
Original w/tank & bell
Gene Floyd

Late 1950's Columbia
Restored
Jerrell Little

1969 Columbia "Mad Mach"
Original
Dan Lepro

1969 Columbia "SS Five"
Original
Dan Lepro

1970 Columbia Twosome Tandem
26", Original
Richard West

1898 Dayton Racer,
Manufactured by
The Davis Sewing Machine Co.,
Serial # 7620.
Daniel Dahlquist

1930's Dayton
Victor Agnew

1935 Dayton
Original
Steve Castelli

1940 Dayton "Dixie Flyer"
Custom Made
Jim Poyneer

Pre-War Dayton – 26"
Nic Frising
The Old Bicycle Shoppe

1940 Dayton Champion Single Flex w/headlights
in tank & electric taillight, Original
Dave Ohrt

1940 Dayton Champion
Restored
Steve Castelli

1940-41 Dayton-Firestone
w/blue tires, Original except for tank.
Don W. Jensen

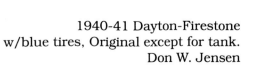

1941 Dayton
Steve Castelli

Dayton Dial-A-Ride
Original
Steve Castelli

1920's Elgin Motorbike
28" Single Tube
Dan Lepro

1933 Elgin
Restored – Nathan Kinsey in Picture
Alan Kinsey

1937 Elgin
26"
Romeo Ghamo

1937 Elgin Custom
Boardwalk Cruiser
Quas Gandolfo

1938 Elgin
Restored
Brad Guilford

1938 Elgin Oriole
26", Original
Bill Waltzer

1938-39 Elgin Twin 20
26", Fully Restored
Bill Waltzer

1938 Elgin Bluebird
Original Paint
Was told this is one of five of these bikes known!
Dave Ohrt

1939 Elgin w/tool box tank
Brad Guilford

1939 Elgin
Restored
M.T. Matthews

1939 Elgin Zoot Suiter
CyclArt

1939 Elgin Bluebird
Steve Castelli

1940 Elgin 4-Star
Girls Sport Model
All Original
Bill Waltzer

1940 Elgin-Firestone Pilot
Brad Guilford

71

1940 Elgin 4-Star Deluxe Twin Bar
w/ accessories
Alan Wentzell

1940 Elgin 4-Star Deluxe
As Found
26" Balloon Tire
Dan Lepro

1940 Elgin
Original
Steve Castelli

1940 Elgin 4-Star
Original
26" Balloon
Dan Lepro

1940 Elgin
Original
Larry Helfand

1941 Elgin-Sears
26"
Romeo Ghamo

Elgin
Herschel Siler

1941 Elgin
Original
Donald Vaughn

Elgin Skylark
Steve Castelli

1953 Firestone
"Dyna-Cycle"
Original
26" Balloon
Dan Lepro

1950's Firestone 500
100% Original
Ralph & Tina Licon

Late 1950's Firestone Speed Cruiser "880"
Middleweight
Original
Nic Frising
The Old Bicycle Shoppe

Firestone Speed Cruiser Deluxe
As New - cardboard is still in light,
battery has never been installed.
Jerrell Little

1886 Gormley & Jeffrey Ordinary, 54"
James & Jamie Allen

1888 Gormley & Jeffrey American Light
Roadster, 56", All Original w/Lucas King of
the Road Hub Lamp No. 129, nickel, 1886.
Peggy Mueller

1891 Gormley & Jeffrey Rambler
w/warning whistle mounted on neck.
Mannikin dates pre 1900's and
has cast iron shoes, "Ouch".
Dave Ohrt

1916 Hawthorne Deluxe Flyer
Restored
Laszlo Palos

1936 Hawthorne Zep
Restored
Steve Castelli

1937 Hawthorne Wingbar
Donald Vaughn

1937 Hawthorne Zep (Ladies)
Restored
26" Balloon
Dan Lepro

1937 Hawthorne Zep (Men's)
Restored
26" Balloon
Dan Lepro

1939 Hawthorne Zep
Steve Castelli

Pre-War Hawthorne, 26"
Restored
Owner: Bob Blansett
Restored by: Nic Frising,
The Old Bicycle Shoppe

1941 Hawthorne, 26"
Restored
Owner: Irene Blansett
Restored by: The Old Bicycle Shoppe

1948 Hawthorne Deluxe Rollfast
26"
Romeo Ghamo

1948 Hawthorne
26", Restored
Regis Hampton

Late 1940's Hawthorne
Ralph & Tina Licon

1949 Hawthorne Deluxe
Steve Doan

1950's Hawthorne All American
Original
M.T. Matthews

1952 Hawthorne-Wards
Completely Original
Bob Harton

1953 Hawthorne
26"
Nancy Frising

1940 Huffman Twin-Flex "Davis Flyer" (1 of 2 known)
All Original, Selected to be in the "Huffy Bicycle Company 100 Years of Excellence" Oct, 1992. Represent-
ing 1 of 14 bikes displayed
Patric Cafaro

80

1941 Huffman
Original
Hugh Rosenweig

1941 Huffman Mainliner
Original
Larry Helfand

1942 Huffman
26", Gliding Ride Spring Fork
Romeo Ghamo

1940 Huffy (Boys)
20"
Richard West

1948 Huffman Indian
Don W. Jensen

1950 Huffy Custom Liner
26"
Romeo Ghamo

1955 Huffy Custom Liner
26"
Romeo Ghamo

1955 Huffy Radio Bike
Original
Don W. Jensen

1956 Huffy Radio Bike
N.O.S.
Steve Castelli

1915 Iver Johnson "Rough Life"
Kent & Sarah Olson

1930's Iver Johnson
Original
26" Balloon
Bill Waltzer

1936 Iver Johnson Motobike
Original
26" Balloon
Dan Lepro

1937 Iver Johnson Arch Frame
Imitation wood grain wheels, The
Wildcat, siren & wire spoke protec-
tors were originally on this bike.
John C. Gordon

1937 Iver Johnson
Chris Roscoe

1940 Iver Johnson
100% Original
Dave Ohrt

1940 Iver Johnson
Original
Donald Vaughn

1941 Iver Johnson
Original
Donald Vaughn

1948 J. C. Higgins
Original (except tail light lens)
Gary DeDontney

1949 J. C. Higgins
Original
Jerrell Little

1950's J. C. Higgins
Jerrell Little

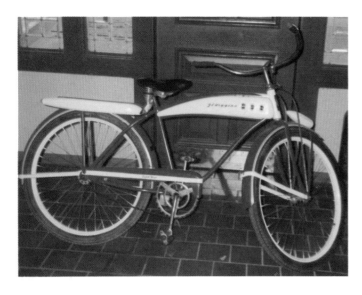

1950 J. C. Higgins Deluxe 26"
Restored
Nic Firsing
The Old Bicycle Shoppe

1950 J. C. Higgins
Original
Don W. Jensen

1951 J. C. Higgins
Don W. Jensen

1951 J. C. Higgins Color Flow
26" Balloon, Restored
(1 of Pair)
Dan Lepro

1951 J. C. Higgins Color Flow
26" Balloon, Restored
(2nd of Pair)
Dan Lepro

1951 J. C. Higgins Regal Deluxe
Original
Gary DeDontney

1951 J. C. Higgins
Color Flow – 26"
Romeo Ghamo

1953 J. C. Higgins Color Flow
Restored
Charles Towagon

1953 J. C. Higgins
Original
Hugh Rosensweig

1955 J. C. Higgins
Turn Signal Model
Victor Agnew

1956 J. C. Higgins
24" – (Nora DeDontney – 8 yrs. old)
Gary DeDontney

1956 J. C. Higgins
26" – Deluxe
Romeo Ghamo

1956 J. C. Higgins Jet Flow
Don W. Jensen

1956 J. C. Higgins
Original
Steve Castelli

1956 Stebler Built for J. C. Higgins
(Built by Stebler Germany for 1 year only)
26" Balloon – Original
Dan Lepro

1957 J. C. Higgins
Boys 26" – All Original
Bill Waltzer

1957 J. C. Higgins
26" – Sealed Boom Headlight
Brad Guilford

1958 J. C. Higgins
24" Flightliner
Brad Guilford

1959 J. C. Higgins
Flightliner – Restored
Paul Popp

1961 J. C. Higgins
Flightliner 26"
Diamond Jubilee
Romeo Ghamo

J. C. Higgins
Model 502
Jesse W. Peoples

1917 Smith Motor Wheel
Ray Daniels

1936 Manton & Smith
Original – 26" Balloon
Dan Lepro

1939 Manton & Smith
Golden Zephyr – Restored
Steve Castelli

1940 Manton & Smith
Golden Zephyr – Original
Donald Vaughn

1918 Mead Ranger
Eddie Jew

1922 Mead Pathfinder
Original – 28" Wood Rims
Wally Lauer

(Approximately) 1925 Mead Pathfinder
Original (even the tires)
Elery L. Beale

1939 Ranger
Original
Bob Nichols

1939 Mercury
by Western Flyer
Brad Guilford

1939 Mercury
Donald Vaughn

1939 Mercury Deluxe
Steve Castelli

1941 Mercury
Original
Steve Castelli

1935 Silver King
Original – 24"
Nic Frising
The Old Bicycle Shoppe

1935 Silver King
Original
Larry Helfand

1935-36 Silver King
Flo-Cycle by Monark
24" Balloon
Dan Lepro

1937 Silver King M-37
Original
Larry Helfand

1937 Silver King
James & Jamie Allen

1937 Monark
Silver King
Original Flocycle
Hugh Rosensweig

1941 Pre-War Monark
26" Dual Spring Two-Speed with
Crossbar Mount Shift Lever
Original
Nic Frising
The Old Bicycle Shoppe

1941 Monark – "Reggie McNamaru
Original
Nic Frising
The Old Bicycle Shoppe

1946 Monark Rocket
Kent & Sarah Olson

1947 Monark
x-Tubo – Custom
oardwalk Cruiser.
Quas Gandolfo

1948 Ladies Monark Deluxe
Original – 26" Horn Tank
Paul Cruz

1949 Monark Super-Twin
Original – 26"
Nic Frising
The Old Bicycle Shoppe

1950's Monark
Original
Jerrell Little

1950's Monark Firestone
Original
Larry Helfand

Early 1950's Monark Super Deluxe
Original Paint
Ty Cutkomp

1950 Monark Super Deluxe
Original
Gary DeDontney

1951 Monark
Gene Autry
Don Jensen

1951 Monark Super Deluxe
Restored
Jim Agan

1951 Monark Rocket
Restored – 26"
Nic Frising
The Old Bicycle Shoppe

1952 Monark Super Deluxe
Victor Agnew

1952 Monark Firestone
Super Cruiser – 26"
Donna Rhymers

1952 Monark Super Deluxe
Original – 26"
Nic Frising
The Old Bicycle Shoppe

1953 Monark Super Deluxe
Original
Bob Harton

1953 Monark Firestone
Super Cruiser
Chuck Cook

1954 Monark Super Deluxe
Donald Vaughn

1955 Monark Firestone
Original
Steve Castelli

1958 Monark Zephyr
Original
Nic Frising
The Old Bicycle Shoppe

1953-1955 Murray Aero-Line
Original
Dan Lepro

1960's Murray AMC VIII
Original – 26"
M.T. Matthews

1970's Murray Chopper
20"
Mike Riach

1900 Pierce
M.T. Matthews

1915 Pierce Roadster
Original
Daniel Dahlquist

1900's Racycle – Track Bike
Designed to set speed records.
The gear ratio is 156 (like riding a 13 foot high wheel)
Steve Carter

1914 Racycle
Model 152
Brad Guilford

Late 1930's Roadmaster
Restored – 26"
Regis Hampton

1941 Roadmaster
Restored
Dan W. Jensen

1948 Roadmaster
Restored
Hugh Rosensweig

1948 Roadmaster
Restored
Hugh Rosensweig

1948-1950 Roadmaster
Cleveland Welding – 26"
Romeo Ghamo

Late 1950's Roadmaster
by A.M.F.
Restored
Gene Floyd

1950 Roadmaster
by Cleveland and Welding
26" Boys Model 19
Restored
Gene Floyd

1952 Roadmaster – 26" Mens
by Cleveland Welding Co.
Restored
Dave Weiler

1952 Roadmaster Luxury Liner
Original
Don W. Jensen

1952 Roadmaster
Luxury Liner
Don W. Jensen

1955 Roadmaster
Luxury Liner
Restored
Hugh Rosensweig

1955 Roadmaster Jr.
Original
Bob Harton

1963 Roadmaster
Sky Rider – 26"
Romeo Ghamo

1965 Roadmaster
Jet Pilot
Brad Guilford

Roadmaster "Mickey Mouse" Bike
16" Tires – Original
Nic Frising
The Old Bicycle Shoppe

1927 Rollfast
Original
John Wallick

1935 Rollfast
Original
Steve Castelli

1936 Rollfast
Original (with toolbox)
Dave Ohrt

1937 Rollfast
Original
Steve Castelli

1939 Rollfast
Restored
Steve Castelli

1941 Rollfast "Ben Hur"
Original – 26"
Pictured is Whitney Frising (Grandaughter)
Nic Frising
The Old Bicycle Shoppe

1942 Rollfast
Original
Elery L. Beale

1948 Rollfast
Restored – 26" Girls
Gene Floyd

1950 Rollfast
Original
Larry Helfand

1950's Rollfast Deluxe – 26"
Romeo Ghamo

1951 Rollfast
Original
Don W. Jensen

1955 Rollfast
Original
Hugh Rosensweig

1956 Rollfast
Original – 20" Girls
Paul R. Grimshaw

1958 Rollfast
Original – 24"
Nic Frising
The Old Bicycle Shoppe

1959 Rollfast
Original
Hugh Rosensweig

1951 Rollfast
20" – Hopalong Cassidy
Don W. Jensen

Hopalong Cassidy – Rollfast
26" Boys
Steve Castelli

Hopalong Cassidy – Rollfast
26" Girls
Steve Castelli

Rollfast – Hopalong Cassidy
24"
Steve Castelli

Schwinn Jaguar Mark II
Original
Don W. Jensen

Schwinn Custom Peapicker
16" Rear – 12" Front
Pictured is owner Dustin Riach

Schwinn Stingray
Original – 5 speed
Nic Frising
The Old Bicycle Shoppe

Schwinn Run-a-bout – 20"
Donald Vaughn

Schwinn Stingray Super Deluxe
Original
Nic Frising
The Old Bicycle Shoppe

Pre-War Schwinn
Truss Bridge – Original
Don Lepro

Custom Built Schwinn
Stingray – 5 speed Tandem
Bob Harton

Schwinn "Custom"
Springer – 20"
Restored
M.T. Matthews

1920 Schwinn Packard
Original – 28"
Nic Frising
The Old Bicycle Shoppe

Mid 1930's Schwinn Hollywood
Restored
M. T. Matthews

1930's Schwinn Liberty
Original
M. T. Matthews

1931 Schwinn Moto-bike
Original – 28"
Alan Kinsey

1932 Schwinn Moto-bike
Original
Elery L. Beale

1934 Schwinn Aerocycle
Original Paint
Dave Ohrt

1934 Schwinn Aerocycle
Restored
Bob Harton

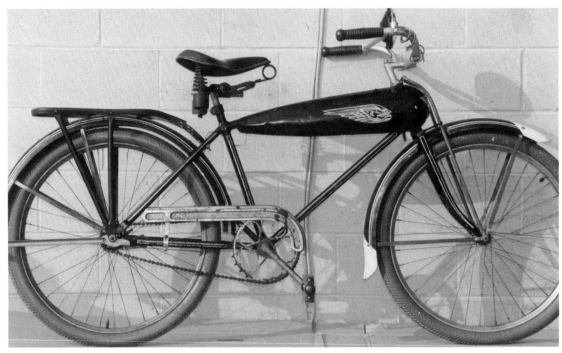

1934-35 Schwinn
Aerocycle
Quas Gandolfo

1935 Schwinn Ranger
Original
Steve Castelli

1936 Schwinn
Auto Cycle
Original
Quas Gandolfo

1936 Schwinn Motorbike
Original
Rare with Jeweled Tank
Bob Harton

1936 Schwinn Ace Moto-bike
Brad Guilford

1936 Schwinn LaSalle
Original
Chicago Cycle Supply
Ken & Marta Magee

1936-37 Schwinn Excelsior
Model C107 – 26" Balloon
Dan Lepro

1937 Schwinn
Spitfire – C-Mod
Christmas Speci
Quas Gandolfo

1937 Mead Rangel
Schwinn Motorbike
Original
Quas Gandolfo

1937 Schwinn Mead Cycle Co.
Ranger Zephyr
Original
Ken & Marta Magee

1937 Schwinn Spartan
Original – 26" Ladies
Dave Weiler

1937 Schwinn Autocycle
Original
Dan Fitzgerald

1938 Schwinn Motorbike
(partially) Restored
Alan Kinsey

1938 Schwinn Moto-bike
Original
Quas Gandolfo

1938 Schwinn
C Model
Daniel Dahlquist

1938 Schwinn Paramount
Serial # A435
Original – Track Bicycle
(1st Year of Paramount)
Daniel Dahlquist

1938 Schwinn
Autocycle
Steve Castelli

1939 Schwinn Auto Cycle
Eddie Jew

1939 Schwinn Motorbike
Original
Ken & Marta Magee

1939 Schwinn DX
with Chicago Cycle
Supply Side Car
Bob Harton

1939 Schwinn DX
Original – 26" Balloon
Mike Ruffing

1939 Schwinn Cycle Track
Original
Bill Waltzer

1940 Schwinn Special
Joe's 50 Year Chicago Flyer
Original – 26" Balloon
Dan Lepro

1940 Schwinn DX – Ladies
Original
Ken & Marta Magee

1940 Schwinn DX
Mead Cycle Co. Crusader
Original
Ken & Marta Magee

1940-41 Schwinn World
Original – 26" – 1 1/4" Tires
Dan Lepro

Early 1940's Schwinn
with 50's Spring Fork
Terry Muellner

1940 Schwinn Ace
Original
Donald Vaughn

1941 Schwinn DX
The World
Chuck Cook

1941 Schwinn Autocycle
Original
Bob Nichols

1941 Schwinn LaSalle
Original
Alan Kinsey

1941 Schwinn B-6
American Flyer
Ken Osman

1942 Schwinn
New World WWII – Defence Model
Original
Daniel Dahlquist

1945 Schwinn Whizzer
Steve Castelli

1947 Schwinn Lincoln
Original – 26" Ladies
Dave Weiler

1947 Schwinn B-6
Restored
Jim Gallagher

1947 Schwinn Autocycle
Steve Doan

1947 Schwinn Standard Autocycle
Original
Quas Gandolfo

1947 Schwinn Excelsior
Original
Quas Gandolfo

1948 Schwinn Whizzer
Restored – J. Engine
John Wallick

1948 Schwinn
Original
Hugh Rosenweig

1948 Schwinn DX
5 Speed Fun Bike
Ralph & Tina Licon

1948 Schwinn Liberty
Original
Laszlo Palos

Early 1948 Schwinn
B607 – Restored
Jim Blum

1948 Schwinn Dynacycle
Restored – 26"
Ray Harper

1948 Schwinn Autocycle
Original – 26" Balloon
Mike Ruffing

1949 Schwinn Tornado
Paul Popp

49 Schwinn B-6
Restored
Quas Gandolfo

139

1950 Schwinn
Girls
Ray Albert

1950 Schwinn Hornet
Original (except seat)
Gary DeDontrey

1950 Schwinn Hornet
26"
Romeo Ghamo

1950 Schwinn
Restored
Laszlo Palos

Late 1950's Schwinn
Deluxe Hornet
Kent & Sarah Olson

1950's Schwinn B-6 Boys
(knee action & lock fork)
Richard West

1950 Schwinn Spitfire
Original paint – 20"
Elery L. Beale

1950's Schwinn
26" Corvette – Girls 3 speed
Restored
Gene Floyd

Early 1950's Schwinn B-6
Victor Agnew

1950's Schwinn Jaguar
Restored
Ralph & Tina Licon

Late 1950's Schwinn Jaguar
Original
Jerrell Little

1950 Schwinn Panther
Original
Quas Gandolfo

1950 Schwinn Panther
Restored – 26"
Dee Riach

Early 1950's Schwinn Panther
Victor Agnew

1950's Schwinn Panther
Don W. Jensen

Late 1950's Panther II
Original
John C. Gordon

1951 Schwinn Panther
Original
Bob Nichols

1951 Schwinn Deluxe Hornet
Restored – 26" Mens
Dave Weiler

1951 Red Phantom
Original
Steve Castelli

1951 Schwinn
BF Goodrich Starlet
Original
Jeff Meyers

1951 Schwinn Whizzer
July Special
Ken & Marta Magee

1952 Schwinn Whizzer
Restored – 26" Balloon
Dan Lepro

1952 Schwinn Phantom
Original
Bob Nichols

1952 Schwinn – 24"
(pictured Ian Roscoe)

1952 Schwinn Excelsior
Original
Ralph & Tina Licon

1952 Schwinn Spitfire
Original
M. T. Matthews

1952 Schwinn Panther
Dual Drum Brakes – Cadet Speedo
Restored
Eric R. Parsons

1952 Schwinn Panther
Original
Larry Helfand

1952 Schwinn B-6
Custom Boardwalk
Cruiser – 6 Speed
Hyperglide
Quas Gandolfo

1952 Schwinn
Hornet
Original
Bob Nichols

1952 Schwinn Streamliner
24" Wheel
Jeff Meyers

1953 Schwinn Whizzer on Phantom
Restored
Don W. Jensen

1953 Schwinn Streamliner
Chuck Cook

1953 Schwinn Built Whizzer
Restored
Bob Harton

1953 Schwinn Meteor
Original – 26" Balloon
Dale R. Jennings

1953 Schwinn Panther
Restored
26" Balloon
Dan Lepro

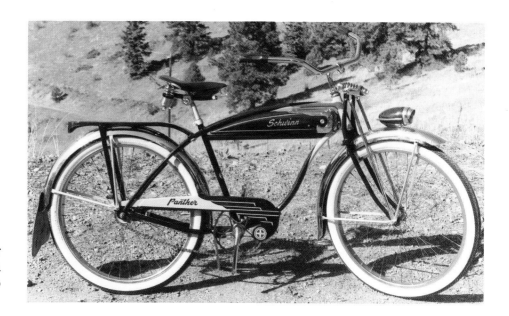

1953 Schwinn Panther
Restored – 26" Balloon
Dan Lepro

1954 Black Phantom
Original
Quas Gandolfo

1954 Schwinn Hornet
B. F. Goodrich – 26"
Romeo Ghamo

1954 Schwinn Green Phantom
Original
Paul R. Grimshaw

1954 Schwinn Whizzer
Original
Eleryl Beale

1955 Schwinn Blue Phantom
Original
Larry Helfand

1955 Schwinn Flying Starlet
Original with
Bendix 2-Speed Shifter
John Wallick

1955 Schwinn Traveler
Original – 26"
Dan Lepro

1956 Schwinn Starlet
Restored – 26"
Dee Riach

153

1956 Schwinn Town &
Country Tandem
CyclArt

1956 Schwinn Wasp
Original – 26"
Larry Fast

1957 Schwinn Corvette
Restored
Boyhood Bicycle
Larry Fast

1957 Schwinn Jaguar Mark II
Original
Bob Harton

1957 Schwinn Spitfire Deluxe
Restored – 26"
Mike Riach

1957 Schwinn Starlet
26"
Brad Guilford

1958 Schwinn Corvette
Original
Hugh Rosensweig

1958 Schwinn Jaguar Mark II
Original
Hugh Rosensweig

1958 Schwinn Starlet
Original – 26"
Mike Riach

1958 Schwinn Straight Bar
Original – 26"
Nic Frising
The Old Bicycle Shoppe

1958 Schwinn Deluxe Tornado
Original
John Wallick

1959 Schwinn Corvette
Restored
Paul Popp

1959 Schwinn Panther III
Custom 10 speeds/disc brakes
Big Banana
Quas Gandolfo

1959 Schwinn Tiger
Original
Hugh Rosensweig

1959 Schwinn
Wasp
Quas Gandolfo

1960's Schwinn Fiesta
Original – 24" Girls
Richard West

1960's Schwinn Typhoon
Original
Ralph & Tina Licon

1960 Schwinn Jaguar Mark IV
(Rare color blue)
Ken Cook

1960 Schwinn Starlet
Original
Bob Nichols

1960 Schwinn
Deluxe Tornado
Original – Boys
John Wallick

1961 Schwinn American
Men's 26"
Ken LeDoux

1962 Schwinn Fleet
Original
Elery Beale

1963 Schwinn Hollywood
Original
(Pictured is Nicole Cramer)
Mike Riach

1963 Schwinn Jaguar
Original – 26"
Mike Riach

1965 Schwinn Fleet
Jeff Meyers

1966 Schwinn Fastback
5-Speed – 1st Production Year
Original
Nelson E. Valosen

1966 Schwinn Panther
Original – 2 Speed
Wally Lauer

1966 Schwinn Super Deluxe Stingray
3 x 3 Three Speed – 20"
Nelson E. Valosen

1967 Stingray Deluxe
20"
Mike Riach

1967 Schwinn Stingray
Ram's Horn Fastback – 20"
Bill Figatner

1968 Schwinn Apple Krate
Original
Nic Frising
The Old Bicycle Shoppe

1968 Schwinn Lemon Peeler
20"
Bill Figatner

1968 Schwinn Mini Twinn
Restored – 20"
Mike Riach

1968 Schwinn Racer
2 Speed Axle – 26" Mens
Dave Weiler

1968 Schwinn Run-A-Bout
Original – 3 Speed Trigger Shift
Nelson E. Valosen

1968 Schwinn Run-A-Bout – 16"
Bill Figatner

1969 Schwinn Apple Krate
Jeff Meyers

1969 Schwinn Fastback
Restored – 3 Speed
Mike Riach

1969 Schwinn Lemon Peeler
Restored – 5 Speed
Mike Riach

1969 Schwinn Lil Tiger
Original
Dan Lepro

1969 Schwinn Pea Picker
20"
Bill Figatner

1970'S Schwinn Bantam
(Convertible Bar)
Richard West

1970's Schwinn Little Tiger
Original paint – 12"
Richard West

1970's Schwinn Custom Paperbox Cruiser
26" Boys
Alan Vaillancourt

1970 Schwinn
Apple Krate – 20"
Bill Figatner

1970 Schwinn Fastback
Original – 20"
Mike Riach

1970 Schwinn Peapicker
Boys 20"
Ken LeDoux

1970 Schwinn
Stingray Fastback
Brad Guilford

1970 Schwinn Typhoon
Custom
Mike Riach

1971 Schwinn Krate-
Cotton Picker Coaster
Jeff Meyers

1971 Schwinn Cotton Picker
Restored – 5 Speed
Mike Riach

1971 Schwinn Deluxe
Stingray – 3 Speed
Jeff Meyers

1971 Grey Ghost
Restored – 5 Speed
Mike Riach

1971 Schwinn Grey Ghost
20" – 5 Speed
Bill Figatner

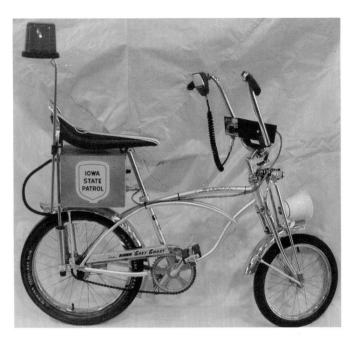

1971 Schwinn
Coaster Brake Grey Ghost
Jim Moss

1971 Schwinn
Orange Krate
Bill Figatner

1971 Schwinn Stingray
3 Speed – 20"
Bill Figatner

1972 Schwinn Apple Krate
Original – 5 Speed – Disk Brake
(Pictured with his bike is Darrell Riach)
Mike Riach

1972 Schwinn Super Deluxe Stingray
2 Speed – 16" – Coaster Brake
Nelson E. Valosen

1973 Schwinn Continental
Original – 10 Speed
Wally Lauer

1973 Schwinn Pixie Stingray
Restored
(Pictured with his bike is Dustin Riach)
Mike Riach

1974 Schwinn Heavy Duty
with Bike Bug Motor – 26"
Nic Frising
The Old Bicycle Shoppe

1974 Schwinn
with Bike Bug Motor
Nic Frising
The Old Bicycle Shoppe

1976 Schwinn Lil Chik
Original – 20"
(Pictured is Tonya Riach with her bike)
Mike Riach

"Going Riding"
(Pictured left: Amanda Cramer and
right: Tonya Riach with their bikes)
Mike Riach

1976 Schwinn Hollywood
Original – 20"
(Pictured is Tonya with her bike)
Mike Riach

1976 Schwinn Hollywood
Original – 20"
(Pictured is Amanda Cramer with her bike)
Mike Riach

1977 Schwinn Heavy Duty
Original – 26"
Nelson E. Valosen

1978 Schwinn Rams Horn Lil Pearl Diver
5 Speed – Disk Brakes – 16"
Nelson Valosen

1979 Schwinn Black Phantom
3 Speed – 26"
Nelson E. Valosen

1979 Schwinn Starlet
3 Speed – 24"
Nelson E. Valosen

1979 Schwinn Stingray II
Original – 20"
Mike Riach

1993 Schwinn Z-Flight
*The Z series was the last
batch of unique juvenile bikes produced by Schwinn while it was run
by the Schwinn family.*
Jeff Meyers

1993 Schwinn Custom Ann Arbor
(Built by Paul Grimshaw)
Bob Harton

1910 Sears Napoleon
28" Wood Rims
Peerless Coaster Brake
Wally Lauer

1960's Sears Spaceliner
Jerrell Little

1960's Sears Spaceliner
Murray
M. T. Matthews

1962 Sears
Spaceliner
Original
Hugh Rosensweig

1965 Sears
Original – 26"
Nic Frising
The Old Bicycle Shoppe

1970's Sears
Front: Screamer Gremlin Coaster
Rear: Spyder 500 – 5 Speed
Jeff Meyers

Pre-War Shelby Supreme
Original – 26"
Nic Frising
The Old Bicycle Shoppe

1910 Shelby Racer
Original
Kerry Holder

1936 Shelby Flyer
Restored – 26" Balloon
Dan Lepro

1936 Shelby Lindy
Restored – 26" Balloon
Dan Lepro

1938 Shelby
Deluxe Flying Cloud
Brad Guilford

1939 Shelby Air Flow
Original
Steve Castelli

1939 Shelby
Original
Donald Vaughn

1939 Shelby
Hiawatha Arrow
Chuck Cook

1941 Shelby Supreme Airflow
Original
Eric R. Parsons

1947 Shelby
Original
Hugh Rosensweig

1947 Shelby Flying Cloud
Original – 26"
Nic Frising
The Old Bicycle Shoppe

1948 Shelby Air Flo Deluxe
Original
Larry Helfand

1949 Shelby Donald Duck Bicycle
Original Store Display
with Animated Donald Duck Rider.
Cardboard Donald "pedals" as rear
wheel goes down.

Photo Courtesy of:
National Bicycle History Archive

1950's Shelby
Original
Gary DeDontney

1950's Shelby Flyers
Original
Jeff Meyers

1950 Shelby Airflow
Original
Bob Nichols

1950's Shelby Flyer
Original Paint
Elery L. Beale

Western Flyer Hi-Lo
Original – 16"
Nic Frising
The Old Bicycle Shoppe

1937 Western Flyer
Made by Cleveland Welding
Restored
Gary DeDontney

1940 Western Flyer
Original
Donald Vaughn

1942 Western Flyer
Brad Guilford

1948 Western Flyer
Made by Cleveland Welding
Original – seat recovered
Gary DeDontney

1950's Western Flyer
Mom & Daughter
Original
Alan Kinsey

1950 Western Flyer Super
Made by Cleveland Welding
Chuck Cook

1955 Western Flyer Super
26" Converted to a 10-Speed
The Old Bicycle Shoppe
Nic Frising

1957 Western Flyer – Made by Monark
Restored – 20" boys
Gene Floyd

1980's Reproduction Western
Flyer – 26" Columbia
Alan Vaillancourt

1963 Western Flyer Cosmic
26"
Romeo Ghamo

1965 Western Flyer
Original – 20"
Richard West

Early 1900's (1902-1908)
Tribune Model 044
Westfield Mfg.
Restored to Original
Bob Harton

1910-1912 Westfield Boy's
28"
Richard West

1917 Westfield Track Bike
Major Taylor
James & Jamie Allen

American Indian Bicycle
26"
American Indian Motorcycle Co., Inc.

Iverson (year unknown)
Original
Jerrell Little

Kent KMX 750
Original
Nelson E. Valosen

Mitsubishi (Made in Occupied Japan)
Heavy Industrial Co. Ltd.
TSU Engineering Works
Joe Carroll

S & K Cycle Mower
Brad Ratliff

Thunder Jet Custom Deluxe
Chain Bike Co.
Bob Harton

1879 Harvard
Made in Coventry England
By Bay Liss Thomas Co.
Restored – 50"
Elery L. Beale

1881 Pope
Original
(Pictured is Kerry Holder)
James D. Holder

1886 Star
52" Wheel
Paul Grimshaw

1886 Victor Light Roadster
56"
Ty Cutkomp

1889 Singer SSS
Mens/Ladies Convertible Tricycle
Steve Carter

1889 Victor Light Roadster
Restored – 54"
Walter Branche

1889 Victor Light Roadster
Ridden by the owner from San Francisco to Boston
in 1984 clocked at speeds over 50mph at Donners
Pass, Sierra, Nevada's elevation 7.088.

1890 Warwick Perfection
Made in Springfield, Mass.
Restored
John T. Dizer

1890 Warwick Perfection
Original
John T. Dizer

1890 Coventry
Made by Coventry Machinist Co.
Coventry England
John T. Dizer

1891 New Mail Light Roadster
Walter Branche

1892 Westminster
James & Jamie Allen

1892-1898 Clipper
Grand Rapids Cycle Co.
Chainless
George Roth

1896 Kenosha with
Solar Kerosene Lamp
Manufactured by Badger
Brass Co. – 28"
Wally Lauer

1897 Lu-mi-num
28"
Alan Kinsey

1897 Alum-min-num
(in script on headpost.)
Donald Vaughn

1897 Old Hickory
Michael Fallon
Copake Country Auction

1897 Humber
American Made Frame #16910
Restored by DeMaus
Daniel Dahlquist

1898 Stearns Ladies Bike
Original Paint & Decals
James & Jamie Allen

1900 Cyclone Racer
M. T. Matthews

1901 Crescent Model 53
CyclArt

1907 Reading Standard
Original – 28"
Dan Lepro

1912 Cyco
Original – 26"
The Old Bicycle Shoppe
Nic Frising

1917 Dexture Teens
Original – with Delta Electric
So. Silver Knight Lantern Pat. 1919
John Wallick

1920 Excelsior
Restored
Michael Fallon
Copake Country Auction

1920 Excelsior
Michigan City, IN
Denis E. Stephen

1920 Indian
Gary Curcio

1920's Thomas English
Muffin Bicycle as used in
commercial TV ad.
James Rothenberger

1920's Trailblazer
The Old Bicycle Shoppe
Nic Frising

1920 Shaw
2 1/2 HP
Richard Griffin

1928 "Lindy" Bicycle – Original
(Supposedly the only one that exists,
with tank in original paint.)
Dave Ohrt

1930's Paris Texas Bike "Rocket"
Brad Ratliff

1935 Trail Blazer
Original – Cleveland Welding Co.
Elery L. Beale

1935 Indian with sidecar
Restored
Bob Nichols

1935 Lovell
26"
Jim Golden

1937 Peerless
Original
Donald Vaughn

1939-40 Cleveland
Welding Deluxe – 26" Balloon
Dan Lepro

201

1940 Perry Cleveland
26"
Romeo Ghamo

1940's Enfield
James & Jamie Allen

1941 Speigel Airmen
Original
Larry Helfand

1950's Stelber
Original – 20"
Nic Frising
The Old Bicycle Shoppe

(This bike was pictured in Volume 1
page 2 of Evolution of the Bicycle.)
This bike was pictured in the Movie
"Sweet Rosie O'Grady" 1943.
Ollie Scheideman

1949 Humber Roadster
(Wheel of Life Sprocket)
Daniel Dahlquist

1956 Simplex Automatic
Original
Nic Frising
The Old Bicycle Shoppe

1960's Open Road Montgomery Ward
Open Road Chopper – 20"
Alan Vaillancourt

Late 1960's – Early 1970's
Swing Bike – Original
John Wallick

1960's Bowden
Spacelander – Original
Jim Gallagher

Reproduction Bowden Spacelander
Bowden Industries
Michael Kaplan

1960 Bowden Spacelander
26"
Paul R. Grimshaw

1961 Mattel Vrroom
Original – 20"
Dan Lepro

1969 Raleigh Chopper
Original
Nic Frising
The Old Bicycle Shoppe

1970's Trail Mate – 3-wheel
Original – 24"
Richard West

1970's Yamaha
BMX Bike Suspension
Quas Gandolfo

1970's Kawasaki
Aluminum BMX Bike
Original
Quas Gandolfo

1977 Easy Rider
Original
Jeff Meyers

Early 1980's Le-Run Scooter
Alan Vaillancourt

Early 1980's Alenbx T-1000 Transbar
Power Bike – Touring Model – 27"
Alan Vaillancourt

1980's Cheeto's Cheezey Rider
24" – Manufactured for
Cheeto's Prize Giveaway by Columbia
Alan Vaillancourt

1990 Frito's Bike – Frito Lay
Promotional Bike Contest Winner
"It Ain't Easy Being Cheesy"
Dan Lepro

1988 Strida Folding Bike
Paul R. Grimshaw

1990 Worksman Downhill Cruiser
3-Speed – Custom Boardwalk Cruiser
Quas Gandolfo

Whizzer Racer with
Harley type bike front fork
and racing saddle.
Ray Spangler

BORED OUT RACER "WIDOWMAKER"

Racing Whizzer
Widowmaker
Ray Spangler

1950 Whizzer –
Pacemaker
Restored
Hugh Rosensweig

Straight Bar Beater Schwinn
with Whizzer Kit
(set up to film Whizzer Rides)
Ray Spangler

Whizzer – Schwinn
with chrome tank
Ray Spangler

1989 Batmobile
10"
Michael Johnson Ghamo

Small Child's Ordinary
(Steel Wheels)
James & Jamie Allen

1940's Child's Bike (maker unknown)
12" – Hard Tires – Front Wheel Drive
Richard West

Vagabond (probably made by Monarch)
16" – Mostly Original
(Folding or two-piece)
Richard West

1880's Child's Highwheel Bicycle
40" Wheel
Ty Cutkomp

Built by Lionel Adams
Customed "Jaunter"

1862-1863 Built by L. Bolender
Delaware, OH
Original
Wally Lauer

All wood 1/2 scale bike.
Replica of 1986, Trek 520
Jim Agan

(Two different) Reproductions
by the Spillanes
Jim Spillane

1960 Reproduction
Ordinary 48" M-2
Engineering, St. Louis, MO
James & Jamie Allen

Hopeless Collectors Garage!!!
Mike Riach

1950's Eagle Reproduction
48" Brand Name "Bone Shaker"
James & Jamie Allen

We bought an old business building that used to be a bike
shop. Guess what we found in the basement! I've been a bike
collector ever since and have been adding to the pile. (1900's
to 1963).
The Old Bicycle Shoppe
Nic Frising

I've gotta stop going to those bike swap meets. "What a bargain".
Don Lepro

Why can't I use the garage?
Romeo Ghamo

1816 Hobby Horse Recreation.
Notice the early bikes had no pedals.
Steve Carter

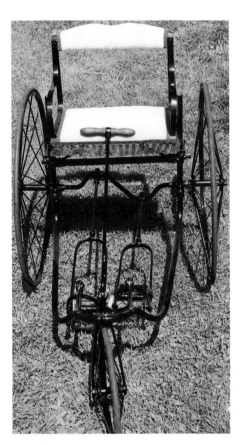

Fairy Tricycle – Late 1890's
by Northington Company
Charlie & Courtney Fisher

"Crazy Cruiser Crawl"
Philadelphia 1991.
Art Museum Rest Stop.
Quas Gandolfo

1886 Loop Frame Tricycle
Steve Carter

1950's-1960's Ice Cream Bike
Original – 26" Balloon
Dan Lepro

1970's Muscle Scooter
Hand-Powered
Alan Vaillancourt

1930's Belt Drive Bike
Kent & Sarah Olson

1910 Exercise Bicycle
Made in Hammond, Indiana
James & Jamie Allen

1890's 5¢ Trade Bicycle.
Stimulator (Rare)
Made by The Sun Mfg., Co.
(Note coin slot upper right).
Dave Ohrt

1940's Columbia
Advertisement Chalkboard.
James & Jamie Allen

Oldest known cycling trophy or
award silver cup inscribed time
1:37. Silver cup on by William W.
Allen at the Velocipede Race on
January 20, 1969.
Walter Branche

From Huffy 100 Show.
Patric Cafaro

Early 1900's Electric Bicycle
Lamp Sign – 8" x 12"
James & Jamie Allen

Advertising Sign –
36" x 12"
Michael Fallon
Copake Country Auction

1888 St. George New York
Bicycle Club Photograph.
Walter Branche

London Street Sign – 23 x 21 – 46 lbs., cast iron.
Circa 1887, oldest bicycle warning sign known.
Walter Branche

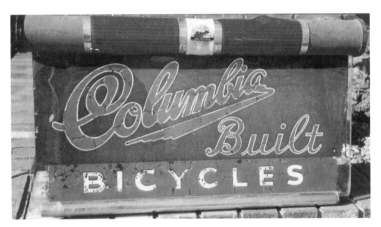

Columbia Built Bicycle painted sign,
lighted, reverse on glass.
James & Jamie Allen

Columbia Bicycles Parts and
Repairs sign – 18" diameter.
James & Jamie Allen

Steins, Cups, bottles and glass bicycle memorabilia.
Steve Carter

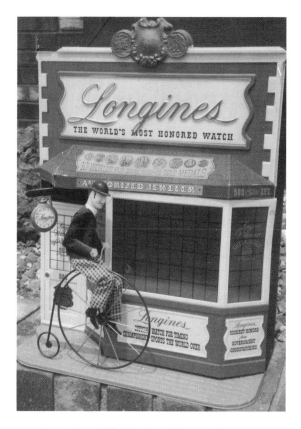

Longines Watch Display with man
on an early highwheel riding past.
James & Jamie Allen

Bicycle engraved watches from
1882 to 1896. (The Highwheel Watch
is a stopwatch and time used in New
Jersey for racing.) Dated and signed
1882.
Walter Branche

1950's Motorol Bike Radio (Rare)
Eddie Jew

1950's Store Display for
Schwinn Tires.
Mike Riach

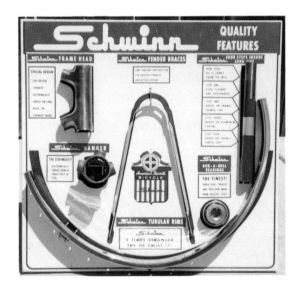

1960's Store Display for
assorted Schwinn parts.
Mike Riach

Master Bike Locks Display.
James & Jamie Allen

Miss Whistles, Bell, Toils, Locks,
Oilers, Pant Guards, "Victor" Alcohol
Torch, Odometers, etc.
Steve Carter

Bike Lamps from 1870-1920 (L to R)
Candle – G&J box type kerosene
Pair of Columbia tricycle lamps
Nickle plated safety bike lamp
High wheel hub light
Safety bike lamp
Steve Carter

Badges that go on front of bikes.
Alan Kinsey

1820's Bicycle Print – original water color.
Ladies Swift Walker.
Walter Branche

1819 Early Hobby Horse Traveler – water color.
Walter Branche

1870's Velocipede Artwork
Original (Rare) – water color.
Walter Branche

1870's Velocipede Artwork
Original (Rare) – water color.
Walter Branche

Columbia Bicycle and Tire Sign
James & Jamie Allen

Columbia Built Bicycles Brass Stencil
14" x 18" framed.
Michael Fallon
Copake Country Auction

Price Guide

The bicycles in this book have been priced by their owners, so you must realize that **ALL** prices are negotiable.

PAGE 41
Sheet Music – $10+

PAGE 46
Top – $3-6
Bottom – $3-6

PAGE 47
Top – $3-6
Bottom – $3-6

PAGE 48
Book – Rare
Photo – $30-40

PAGE 49
Top *(AMF Roadmaster)* – $200
Middle Left *(AMF Royal Master)* – $250+
Middle Right *(B.F. Goodrich)* – $600-800
Bottom *(B.F. Goodrich Challenger)* – $300

PAGE 50
Top *(B.F. Goodrich Challenger)* – $200
Middle *(Colson-Evans)* – $500
Bottom Left *(Colson Tricycle)* – $200
Bottom Right *(Colson Tandem)* – $400+

PAGE 51
Top *(Colson Flyer)* – $800
Middle *(Colson Aristocrat)* – $2500+
Bottom *(Colson)* – $2000+

PAGE 52
Top *(Colson Commander)* – $2500+
Middle Left *(Colson-Goodyear Clipper)* – $2000
Middle Right *(Colson-Firestone Super Cruiser)* – $4000
Bottom *(Colson Imperial)* – $4000+

PAGE 53
Top *(Colson Tandem)* – $1200+
Middle *(Colson Twin Cushion)* – $3500+
Bottom *(Colson)* – $800

PAGE 54
Top *(Colson Lady Clipper)* – $1050
Middle Right *(Colson-Evans)* – $250
Middle Left *(Colson Cadet)* – $300
Bottom *(Colson-Evans)* – $200

PAGE 55
Top *(Colson-Evans)* – $75
Middle Left *(Columbia Expert)* – $4000
Middle Right *(Columbia Light Roadster)* – $2800
Bottom Left *(Columbia Light Roadster)* – $2500+
Bottom Right *(Columbia Tandem Tricycle)* – $18,000-22,000

PAGE 56
Top Left *(Columbia Light Roadster)* – $4500
Top Right *(Columbia Expert Ordinary)* – Reference only
Middle *(Columbia)* – $500
Bottom *(Columbia Springer)* – $3500+

PAGE 57
Top *(Columbia Motobike)* – $700
Middle *(Columbia Air-Rider)* – $3500+
Bottom *(Columbia Twin Bar)* – $3000

PAGE 58
Top *(Columbia)* – $900
Middle *(Columbia Superb)* – $2800
Bottom *(Columbia)* – $4500+

PAGE 59
Top *(Columbia Superb F9T)* – $1500+
Middle Left *(Columbia U.S. Army)* – $1200+
Middle Right *(Columbia)* – $800
Bottom *(Columbia)* – $1000

PAGE 60
Top *(Columbia 5-Star Superb)* – $2200
Middle *(Columbia 5-Star Deluxe)* – $1250
Bottom *(Columbia 5-Star)* – $1800

PAGE 61
Top *(Columbia 5-Star Supreme)* – $1600
Middle *(Columbia 5-Star)* – $500
Bottom *(Columbia w/Racycle nameplate)* – $500

PAGE 62
Top *(Columbia 5-Star)* – $900
Middle *(Columbia 5-Star Super)* – $1800
Bottom *(Columbia)* – $700+

PAGE 63
Top *(Columbia)* – $300
Middle *(Columbia)* – $300+
Bottom *(Columbia Mad March)* – $300

PAGE 64
Top *(Columbia SS Five)* – $450
Middle *(Columbia Twosome Tandem)* – $100
Bottom *(Dayton Racer)* – Rare

PAGE 65
Top *(Dayton)* – $800-1000
Middle *(Dayton)* – $3500+
Bottom *(Dayton Dixie Flyer)* – Reference only
                        owner asking – $2000+

PAGE 66
Top Left *(Dayton)* – $850+
Top Right *(Dayton Champion)* – $1100+
Middle *(Dayton Champion)* – $4500+
Bottom *(Dayton-Firestone)* – $1000

PAGE 67
Top *(Dayton)* – $3500+
Middle *(Dayton Dial-A-Ride)* – $4000+
Bottom *(Elgin Motorbike)* – $300

PAGE 68
Top Left *(Elgin)* – $4000
Top Right *(Elgin)* – $400
Middle *(Elgin Custom)* – $750+
Bottom *(Elgin)* – $1700

PAGE 69
Top *(Elgin)* Oriole – $800+
Middle *(Elgin Twin)* – $1000+
Bottom *(Elgin Bluebird)* – Rare

PAGE 70
Top *(Elgin)* – Reference only
Middle *(Elgin)* – $650+
Bottom *(Elgin Zoot Suiter)* – $3500

PAGE 71
Top *(Elgin Bluebird)* – $10,000+
Middle *(Elgin 4-Star)* – $650+
Bottom *(Elgin-Firestone Pilot)* – $1500+

PAGE 72
Top Left *(Elgin 4-Star Deluxe)* – $800+
Top Right *(Elgin 4-Star Deluxe)* – $1000
Middle *(Elgin)* – $1500+
Bottom *(Elgin 4-Star)* - $500

PAGE 73
Top *(Elgin)* – $900

Middle Left *(Elgin-Sears)* – $175
Middle Right *(Elgin)* – Limited Information available
Bottom *(Elgin)* – $1400

PAGE 74
Top *(Elgin Skylark)* – $2500+
Middle *(Firestone Dyna-Cycle)* – $3500
Bottom Left *(Firestone 500)* – $300+
Bottom Right *(Firestone Speed Cruiser 880)* – $250+

PAGE 75
Top *(Firestone Speed Cruiser Deluxe)* – $600+
Middle Left *(Gormley & Jeffrey Ordinary)* – $3500
Middle Right *(Gormley & Jeffrey American Light)* – $3000+
Bottom *(Gormley & Jeffrey Rambler)* – $1800+

PAGE 76
Top *(Hawthorne Deluxe Flyer)* – $1100
Middle *(Hawthorne Zip)* – $3500+
Bottom *(Hawthorne Wingbar)* – $4500

PAGE 77
Top *(Hawthorne Zep Ladies)* – $1800
Middle *(Hawthorne Zep Men's)* – $2500
Bottom *(Hawthorne Zep)* – $4500+

PAGE 78
Top *(Pre-War Hawthorne)* – $750+
Middle *(Hawthorne)* – $650+
Bottom *(Hawthorne Deluxe Rollfast)* – $900

PAGE 79
Top *(Hawthorne)* – 800+
Middle *(Hawthorne)* – $500+
Bottom *(Hawthorne Deluxe)* – $1000+

PAGE 80
Top *(Hawthorne All American)* – $1000+
Middle *(Hawthorne-Wards)* – $1000+
Bottom Left *(Hawthorne)* – $500+
Bottom Right *(Huffman Twin-Flex Davis Flyer)* – $7500+

PAGE 81
Top Left *(Huffman)* – $800
Top Right *(Huffman Mainliner)* – $3800
Middle Left *(Huffman)* – $900
Middle Right *(Huffy boys)* – $50
Bottom Left *(Huffman Indian)* – $2400+
Bottom Right *(Huffy Custom Liner)* – $150

PAGE 82
Top Left *(Huffy Custom Liner)* – $200

Top Right (*Huffy Radio*) – $3500+
Middle (*Huffy Radio*) – $2500+
Bottom (*Iver Johnson*) – $800+

PAGE 83
Top (*Iver Johnson*) – $750+
Middle (*Iver Johnson Motobike*) – $3000
Bottom (*Iver Johnson*) – $1200+

PAGE 84
Top Left (*Iver Johnson*) – $500
Top Right (*Iver Johnson*) – $2000+
Middle (*Iver Johnson*) – $2500
Bottom (*Iver Johson*) – $1500

PAGE 85
Top (*J.C. Higgins*) – $375
Middle (*J.C. Higgins*) – $300+
Bottom (*J.C. Higgins*) – $600+

PAGE 86
Top (*J.C. Higgins Deluxe*) – $650
Middle (*J.C. Higgins*) – $800
Bottom (*J.C. Higgins*) – $1100

PAGE 87
Top (*J.C. Higgins Color Flow*) – $1500
Middle (*J.C. Higgins Color Flow*) – $2000
Bottom (*J.C. Higgins Regal Deluxe*) – $350

PAGE 88
Top Left (*J.C. Higgins Color Flow*) – $125
Top Right (*J.C. Higgins Color Flow*) – $1500-2000
Middle (*J.C. Higgins*) – $500
Bottom (*J.C. Higgins*) – $800-1000

PAGE 89
Top (*J.C. Higgins*) – $1100
Middle (*J.C. Higgins*) – $600
Bottom (*J.C. Higgins Jet Flow*) – $900

PAGE 90
Top (*J.C. Higgins*) – $1500+
Middle (*Stebler – J.C. Higgins*) – $600
Bottom (*J.C. Higgins*) – $1200+

PAGE 91
Top (*J.C. Higgins*) – $450
Middle (*J.C. Higgins*) – $125
Bottom (*J.C. Higgins*) – $450

PAGE 92
Top (*J.C. Higgins Flightliner*) – $400
Middle (*J.C. Higgins*) – $250
Bottom (*Smith Motor Wheel*) – Rare

PAGE 93
Top (*Manton & Smith*) – $600
Middle (*Manton & Smith Golden Zephyr*) – $4500+
Bottom (*Manton & Smith Golden Zephyr*) – $3000

PAGE 94
Top (*Mead Ranger*) – Reference only
Middle (*Mead Pathfinder*) – $200+
Bottom (*Mead Pathfinder*) – $1200

PAGE 95
Top (*Ranger*) – $800+
Middle (*Mercury*) – $400
Bottom (*Murcury*) – $875

PAGE 96
Top (*Mercury Deluxe*) – $4000+
Middle (*Mercury*) – $1500+
Bottom (*Silver King*) – $450

PAGE 97
Top(*Silver King*) – $1800
Middle (*Silver King Flo-Cycle*) – $1600
Bottom (*Silver King*) – $6500

PAGE 98
Top (*Silver King*) – $450
Middle (*Monark Silver King*) – $2000
Bottom (*Pre-War Monark*) – $850

PAGE 99
Top (*Monark Reggie McNamaru*) – Reference only
Middle (*Monark Rocket*) – $600
Bottom (*Monark Hex-Turbo*) – $900+

PAGE 100
Top (*Monark Deluxe Ladies*) – $400
Middle (*Monark Super-Twin*) – $2500
Bottom (*Monark*) – $800

PAGE 101
Top (*Monark Firestone*) – $1600
Middle (*Monark Super Deluxe*) – $500
Bottom (*Monark Super Deluxe*) – $500

PAGE 102

Top *(Monark)* – $4000+
Middle *(Monark Super Deluxe)* – $2200
Bottom *(Monark Rocket)* – $800+

PAGE 103

Top *(Monark Super Deluxe)* – $800-1200
Middle *(Monark Firestone)* – $1500
Bottom *(Monark Super Deluxe)* – $750

PAGE 104

Top *(Monark Super Deluxe)* – $750+
Middle *(Monark Firestone)* – $1000+
Bottom *(Monark Super Deluxe)* – $1250

PAGE 105

Top *(Monark Firestone)* – $2000+
Middle *(Monark Zephyr)* – $300+
Bottom *(Murray Aero-Line)* – $300

PAGE 106

Top *(Murray AMC VIII)* – $300+
Middle *(Murray Chopper)* – $250
Bottom *(Pierce)* – $900+

PAGE 107

Top *(Pierce Roadster)* – $1000
Middle *(Racycle)* – $1000
Bottom *(Racycle)* – Reference only

PAGE 108

Top *(Roadmaster)* – $350
Middle *(Roadmaster)* – $1400
Bottom *(Roadmaster)* – $600

PAGE 109

Top *(Roadmaster)* – $600
Middle *(Roadmaster)* – $250
Bottom *(Roadmaster)* – $500

PAGE 110

Top *(Roadmaster)* – $750
Middle *(Roadmaster)* – $1500
Bottom *(Roadmaster Luxury Liner)* – $700

PAGE 111

Top *(Roadmaster)* – $1000
Middle *(Roadmaster Luxury Liner)* – $600
Bottom *(Roadmaster Jr.)* – $300+

PAGE 112

Top *(Roadmaster Sky Rider)* – $150
Middle *(Roadmaster Jet Pilot)* – $300
Bottom *(Roadmaster Mickey Mouse)* – Rare

PAGE 113

Top *(Rollfast)* – Reference only
Middle *(Rollfast)* – $1500+
Bottom *(Rollfast)* – $1600+

PAGE 114

Top *(Rollfast)* – $3500+
Middle *(Rollfast)* – $3500+
Bottom *(Rollfast Ben Hur)* – $800

PAGE 115

Top *(Rollfast)* – $3000
Middle *(Rollfast)* – $550
Bottom *(Rollfast)* – $1200

PAGE 116

Top *(Rollfast Deluxe)* – $800
Middle *(Rollfast)* – $550
Bottom *(Rollfast)* – $500

PAGE 117

Top *(Rollfast)* – $350
Middle *(Rollfast)* – $300
Bottom *(Rollfast)* – $500

PAGE 118

Top *(Rollfast)* – $2500+
Middle *(Rollfast – Hopalong Cassidy)* – $2500+
Bottom *(Rollfast – Hopalong Cassidy)* – $2500+

PAGE 119

Top *(Rollfast – Hopalong Cassidy)* – $2500+
Middle *(Schwinn Jaguar Mark II)* – $500
Bottom *(Schwinn Custom Peapicker)* – $300

PAGE 120

Top *(Schwinn Stingray)* – $400
Middle *(Schwinn Run-a-bout)* – $400
Bottom *(Schwinn Stingray Super Deluxe)* – $500

PAGE 121

Top *(Pre-War Schwinn Truss Bridge)* – $400
Middle *(Schwinn Stingray Custom Built)* – $500
Bottom *(Schwinn Custom Springer)* – $900+

PAGE 122
Top (*Schwinn Packard*) – $900
Middle (*Schwinn Hollywood*) – $700+
Bottom (*Schwinn Liberty*) – $400+

PAGE 123
Top (*Schwinn Moto-bike*) – $1500
Middle (*Schwinn Moto-bike*) – $2000
Bottom (*Schwinn Aerocycle*) – $1500+

PAGE 124
Top (*Schwinn Aerocycle*) – $1700+
Middle (*Schwinn Aerocycle*) – $3000+
Bottom (*Schwinn Ranger*) – $3500+

PAGE 125
Top (*Schwinn Auto Cycle*) – $3000+
Middle (*Schwinn Motorbike*) – $3000+
Bottom (*Schwinn Ace Moto-bike*) – Reference only

PAGE 126
Top (*Schwinn LaSalle*) – $1000+
Middle (*Schwinn Excelsior*) – $1200
Bottom (*Schwinn Spitfire*) – $800+

PAGE 127
Top (*Schwinn Mead Rangel Motorbike*) – $1000+
Middle (*Schwinn Ranger Zephyr*) – $1000+
Bottom (*Schwinn Spartan*) – $150

PAGE 128
Top Left (*Schwinn Åutocycle*) – $3000
Top Right (*Schwinn Motorbike*) – $2600
Bottom (*Schwinn Motobike*) – $2000+

PAGE 129
Top (*Schwinn C Model*) – $1500
Middle (*Schwinn Paramount*) – $1500
Bottom (*Schwinn Autocycle*) – $5000+

PAGE 130
Top (*Schwinn Autocycle*) – $5500
Middle (*Schwinn Motorbike*) – $1000+
Bottom (*Schwinn DX w/side car*) – $800+

PAGE 131
Top (*Schwinn DX*) – $1700
Middle (*Schwinn Cycle Track*) – $1000+
Bottom (*Schwinn Special 50 yr. Chicago Flyer*) – $2500

PAGE 132
Top Left (*Schwinn DX*) – $250+
Top Right (*Schwinn DX Crusader*) – $800+
Middle (*Schwinn World*) – $200
Bottom Left (*Schwinn*) – Reference only
Bottom Right (*Schwinn Ace*) – $1700

PAGE 133
Top (*Schwinn DX*) – $1000+
Middle (*Schwinn Autocycle*) – $1200+
Bottom (*Schwinn LaSalle*) – $2200

PAGE 134
Top (*Schwinn B-6 American Flyer*) – $1800
Middle (*Schwinn New WWII Defence Model*) – $300
Bottom (*Schwinn Whizzer*) – $3500+

PAGE 135
Top (*Schwinn Lincoln*) – $400
Middle (*Schwinn B-6*) – $2400
Bottom (*Schwinn Autocycle*) – $1000+

PAGE 136
Top (*Schwinn Standard Autocycle*) – $750+
Bottom (*Schwinn Excelcior*) – $750

PAGE 137
Top (*Schwinn Whizzer*) – Reference only
Middle (*Schwinn*) – $400
Bottom (*Schwinn DX 5-Speed*) – $300+

PAGE 138
Top (*Schwinn Liberty*) – $500
Middle (*Schwinn B607*) – $2500
Bottom (*Schwinn Dynacycle*) – Reference only

PAGE 139
Top (*Schwinn Autocycle*) – $850+
Middle (*Schwinn Tornado*) – $250
Bottom (*Schwinn B-6*) – $2000

PAGE 140
Top (*Schwinn*) – $100
Middle (*Schwinn Hornet*) – $225
Bottom (*Schwinn Hornet*) – $200

PAGE 141
Top (*Schwinn*) – $750
Middle (*Schwinn Deluxe Hornet*) – $750
Bottom (*Schwinn B-6 boys*) – $700

PAGE 142
Top *(Schwinn Spitfire)* – $300
Middle *(Schwinn Corvette)* – $350
Bottom *(Schwinn B-6)* – $800

PAGE 143
Top *(Schwinn Jaguar)* – $500+
Middle *(Schwinn Jaguar)* – $1200
Bottom *(Schwinn Panther)* – $1800+

PAGE 144
Top *(Schwinn Panther)* – $800
Middle *(Schwinn Panther)* – $800-1000
Bottom *(Schwinn Panther)* – $1500

PAGE 145
Top *(Schwinn Panther II)* – $800+
Middle *(Schwinn Panther)* – $1500+
Bottom *(Schwinn Deluxe Hornet)* – $2000

PAGE 146
Top *(Red Phantom)* – $3500+
Middle Left *(Schwinn BF Goodrich Starlet)* – $500+
Middle Right *(Schwinn Whizzer)* – Reference only
Bottom *(Schwinn Whizzer)* – $2500

PAGE 147
Top *(Schwinn Phantom)* – $1800+
Middle Left *(Schwinn)* – $600
Middle Right *(Schwinn Excelsior)* – $600+
Bottom *(Schwinn Spitfire)* – $400+

PAGE 148
Top *(Schwinn Panther)* – $1500+
Middle *(Schwinn Panther)* – $1500+
Bottom *(Schwinn B-6 Custom Boardwalk Cruiser)* – $750+

PAGE 149
Top *(Schwinn Hornet)* – $700+
Middle Left *(Schwinn Streamliner)* – $600+
Middle Right *(Schwinn Whizzer on Phantom)* – $5000
Bottom *(Schwinn Streamliner)* – $500+

PAGE 150
Top *(Schwinn Built Whizzer)* – $2000+
Middle *(Schwinn Meteor)* – $300
Bottom *(Schwinn Panther)* – $1400

PAGE 151
Top *(Schwinn Panther)* – $1600
Middle *(Black Phantom)* – $1800+

Bottom *(Schwinn Hornet)* – $1200+

PAGE 152
Top *(Schwinn Green Phantom)* – $3000
Middle *(Schwinn Whizzer)* – $6000
Bottom *(Schwinn Blue Phantom)* – $2800

PAGE 153
Top *(Schwinn Flying Starlet)* – $300+
Middle *(Schwinn Traveler)* – $400
Bottom *(Schwinn Starlet)* – $500

PAGE 154
Top *(Schwinn Town & Country Tandem)* – $3500
Middle *(Schwinn Wasp)* – $350
Bottom *(Schwinn Corvette)* – $400

PAGE 155
Top *(Schwinn Jaguar Mark II)* – $1000+
Middle *(Schwinn Spitfire Deluxe)* – $500
Bottom *(Schwinn Starlet)* – $250

PAGE 156
Top *(Schwinn Corvette)* – $500
Middle *(Schwinn Jaguar Mark II)* – $700
Bottom *(Schwinn Starlet)* – $200

PAGE 157
Top *(Schwinn Straight Bar)* – $500
Middle *(Schwinn Deluxe Tornado)* – $400+
Bottom *(Schwinn Corvette)* – $400

PAGE 158
Top *(Schwinn Panther III)* – $750+
Middle *(Schwinn Tiger)* – $300
Bottom *(Schwinn Wasp)* – $500

PAGE 159
Top *(Schwinn Fiesta)* – $150
Middle *(Schwinn Typhoon)* – $200+
Bottom *(Schwinn Jaguar Mark IV)* – $600

PAGE 160
Top *(Schwinn Starlet)* – $300+
Middle *(Schwinn Deluxe Tornado)* – $300+
Bottom *(Schwinn American)* – $450

PAGE 161
Top *(Schwinn Fleet)* – $500
Middle *(Schwinn Hollywood)* – $200+
Bottom *(Schwinn Jaguar)* – $700

PAGE 162
Top Left *(Schwinn Fleet)* – $250+
Top Right *(Schwinn Fastback 5-Speed)* – $200+
Middle *(Schwinn Panther)* – $300
Bottom *(Schwinn Super Deluxe Stingray)* – Reference only

PAGE 163
Top *(Schwinn Stingray Deluxe)* – $300
Middle *(Schwinn Stingray Ram's Horn Fastback)* – $500
Bottom *(Schwinn Apple Krate)* – $350

PAGE 164
Top *(Schwinn Lemon Peeler)* – $1200
Middle *(Schwinn Mini Twinn)* – $400
Bottom *(Schwinn Racer)* – $275

PAGE 165
Top Left *(Schwinn Run-A-Bout)* – $600+
Top Right *(Schwinn Run-A-Bout)* – $600-700
Middle Left *(Schwinn Apple Krate)* – $700+
Middle Right *(Schwinn Fastback)* – $200
Bottom *(Schwinn Lemon Peeler)* – $700

PAGE 166
Top Left *(Schwinn Lil Tiger)* – $200
Middle *(Schwinn Pea Picker)* – $700
Bottom *(Schwinn Ban tam)* – $100

PAGE 167
Top *(Schwinn Little Tiger)* – $25+
Middle *(Schwinn Custom Paperbox Cruisrer)* – $350
Bottom Left *(Schwinn Apple Krate)* – $800
Bottom Right *(Schwinn Fastback)* – $150

PAGE 168
Top *(Schwinn Pea Picker)* – $500
Middle *(Schwinn Stingray Fastback)* – $150
Bottom *(Schwinn Typhoon Custom)* – $400

PAGE 169
Top Left *(Schwinn Krate Cotton Picker Coaster)* – $300+
Top Right *(Schwinn Cotton Picker)* – $700
Middle *(Schwinn Deluxe Stingray)* – $600+
Bottom Left *(Schwinn Grey Ghost)* – $800
Bottom Right *(Schwinn Grey Ghost)* – $1200

PAGE 170
Top *(Schwinn Coaster Brake Grey Ghost)* – $1200
Middle *(Schwinn Orange Krate)* – $800
Bottom *(Schwinn Stingray 3-Speed)* – $1000

PAGE 171
Top *(Schwinn Apple Krate)* – $800
Middle *(Schwinn Super Deluxe Stingray)* – $300+
Bottom *(Schwinn Continental)* – $300+

PAGE 172
Top Left *(Schwinn Pixie Stingray)* – $250
Top Right *(Schwinn Heavy Duty w/Bike Bug Motor)* – $500
Middle *(Schwinn with Bike Bug Motor)* – $500+
Bottom *(Schwinn Lil Chik)* – $200

PAGE 173
Top– *(For reference only)*
Middle *(Schwinn Hollywood)* – $100
Bottom *(Schwinn Hollywood)* – $100

PAGE 174
Top *(Schwinn Heavy Duty)* – $200+
Middle *(Schwinn Rams Horn Lil Pearl Driver)* – $500+
Bottom *(Schwinn Black Phantom)* – Reference only

PAGE 175
Top *(Schwinn Starlet)* – $1000+
Middle *(Schwinn Stingray II)* – $150
Bottom Left *(Schwinn Z-Flight)* – $200+
Bottom Right *(Schwinn Custom Ann Arbor)* – Priceless

PAGE 176
Top *(Sears Napoleon)* – $1200+
Middle *(Sears Spaceliner)* – $400+
Bottom *(Sears Spaceliner)* – $600+

PAGE 177
Top *(Sears Spaceliner)* – $700
Middle *(Sears)* – $350
Bottom *(Sears bikes)* – Reference only

PAGE 178
Top Left *(Pre-War Shelby Supreme)* – $400+
Top Right *(Shelby Racer)* – $900-1200
Middle *(Shelby Flyer)* – $2000
Bottom *(Shelby Lindy)* – $1600

PAGE 179
Top *(Shelby Deluxe Flying Cloud)* – $3000
Middle *(Shelby Air Flow)* – $3000+
Bottom *(Shelby)* – $800

PAGE 180
Top *(Shelby Hiawatha Arrow)* – $2000+
Middle *(Shelby Supreme Airflow)* – $2000+
Bottom *(Shelby)* – $800

PAGE 181
Top *(Shelby Flying Cloud)* – $650
Middle *(Shelby Air Flo Deluxe)* – $1200
Bottom *(Shelby Donald Duck)* – Rare

PAGE 182
Top *(Shelby)* – $375
Middle *(Shelby Flyers)* – $800+
Bottom *(Shelby Airflow)* – $750+

PAGE 183
Top *(Shelby Flyer)* – $800
Middle *(Western Flyer)* – $350+
Bottom *(Western Flyer)* – $800

PAGE 184
Top *(Western Flyer)* – $1350
Middle *(Western Flyer)* – $1000
Bottom *(Western Flyer)* – $450

PAGE 185
Top *(West Flyer)* – $300 for pair
Middle *(Western Flyer Super)* – $1500+
Bottom *(Western Flyer Super)* – $1000+

PAGE 186
Top Left *(Western Flyer)* – $400
Top Right *(Western Flyer Reproduction)* – $300
Middle *(Western Flyer Cosmic)* – $200
Bottom *(Western Flyer)* – $50

PAGE 187
Top *(Tribune Model 044)* – $2000
Middle *(Westfield Boy's)* – $100+
Bottom *(Westfield Track Bike)* – $550

PAGE 188
Top *(American Indian)* – $5000+
Middle *(Iverson)* – $250+
Bottom *(Kent KMX 750)* – Reference only

PAGE 189
Top *(Mitsubishi)* – Reference only
Middle *(S & K Cycle Mower)* – Reference only
Bottom *(Thunder Jet Custom Deluxe)* – $500

PAGE 190
Top Left *(Harvard)* – $5000
Top Right *(Pope)* – $5000
Bottom *(Star)* – $10,000

PAGE 191
Top Left *(Victor Light Roadster)* – $3500
Top Right *(Singer SSS)* – $10,000
Middle *(Victor Light Roadster)* – $10,000+
Bottom *(Victor Light Roadster)* – $10,000+

PAGE 192
Top *(Warwick Perfection)* – $250+
Middle *(Warwick Perfection)* – $150+
Bottom *(Coventry)* – $350+

PAGE 193
Top *(New Mail Light Roadster)* – $400+
Middle *(Westminster)* – $1050
Bottom *(Clipper)* – $700+

PAGE 194
Top *(Kenusha)* – $500
Middle *(Lu-mi-num)* – $2500
Bottom *(Alum-min-num)* – $1300

PAGE 195
Top *(Old Hickory)* – $4675
Middle *(Humber)* – $2000
Bottom *(Stearns Ladies Bike)* – $750

PAGE 196
Top *(Cyclone Racer)* – $500+
Middle *(Crescent Model 53)* – $2500
Bottom *(Reading Standard)* – $600

PAGE 197
Top *(Cyco)* – $850+
Middle *(Dexture Teens)* – Reference only
Bottom *(Excelsior)* – $700

PAGE 198
Top *(Excelsior)* – $1500
Middle *(Indian)* – $8500
Bottom *(Thomas English)* – $500+

PAGE 199
Top *(Trailblazer)* – $250
Middle *(Shaw)* – $115
Bottom *(Lindy)* – Rare

PAGE 200
Top *(Paris Texas Bike Rocket)* – $400+
Middle *(Trail Blazer)* – $1000
Bottom *(Indian w/sidecar)* – Rare

PAGE 201
Top *(Lovell)* – $1200
Middle *(Peerless)* – $800
Bottom *(Cleveland)* – $1200

PAGE 202
Top *(Perry Cleveland)* – $100
Middle *(Enfield)* – $275
Bottom *(Speigel Airmen)* – $975

PAGE 203
Top Left *(Stelber)* – $200+
Top Right – Reference only
Middle *(Humber Roadster)* – $350
Bottom *(Simplex Automatic)* – $3500

PAGE 204
Top Left *(Open Road Chopper)* – $400+
Top Right *(Swing Bike)* – $400+
Middle *(Bowden Spacelander)* – $12,000
Bottom *(Reprod. of Bowden Spacelander)* – Reference only

PAGE 205
Top *(Bowden Spacelander)* – $10,000
Bottom Left *(Mattel Vrroom)* – $300
Bottom Right *(Raleigh Chopper)* – $350

PAGE 206
Top *(Trail Mate)* – $200
Bottom *(Yamaha BMX)* – $500

PAGE 207
Top *(Kawasaki BMX)* – $1000
Middle Left *(Easy Rider)* – $250+
Middle Right *(Le-Run Scooter)* – $75
Bottom *(Alenbx T-1000 Transbar Power Bike)* – $500

PAGE 208
Top Left *(Cheeto's Cheezy Rider)* – $400
Top Right *(Frito's Bike)* – $400
Bottom *(Strida Folding Bike)* – $300

PAGE 209
Top *(Worksman Downhill Cruiser)* – $2500+
Bottom *(Whizzer Racer)* – Reference only

PAGE 210
Top *(Racing Whizzer)* – Reference only
Middle *(Whizzer Pacemaker)* – $4000
Bottom *(Straight Bar Beater w/Whizzer kit)* – Reference only

PAGE 211
Top *(Whizzer-Schwinn)* – Reference only
Middle Left *(Batmobile)* – $125
Middle Right *(Child's Ordinary)* – $450
Bottom – $50

PAGE 212
Top Left *(Vagabond)* – $100
Top Right *(Child's Highwheel)* – $1800
Middle *(Customed Jaunter)* – Reference only
Bottom – $4000

PAGE 213
Top *(Replica of 1986 Trek 520)* – Reference only
Middle pictures – reproductions – Reference only
Bottom *(Reproduction Ordinary)* – Reference only
Selling for $700

PAGE 214
Top Left *(Eagle Reproduction)* – Reference only
Selling for $650
Top Right – Collection – Reference only
Bottom – Collection – Reference only

PAGE 215
Top – Collection – Reference only
Middle – Collection – Reference only
Bottom *(Hobby Horse Recreation)* – $1000

PAGE 216
Top Left – Collection – Reference only
Top Right *(Fairy Tricycle)* – $500-1000
Bottom Left *(Loop Frame Tricycle)* – $15,000
Bottom Right *(Ice Cream Bike)* – $800

PAGE 217
Top *(Muscle Scooter)* – $100
Middle *(Belt Drive Bike)* – $150
Bottom *(Exercise Bicycle)* – $250

PAGE 218
Top *(Trade Bicycle Stimulator)* – Reference only
Bottom Left *(Columbia Advertisement Chalkboard)* – $9⌷
Bottom Right *(Cycling Trophy)* – Rare

PAGE 219
Top Left *(Huffy 100 Show)* – Reference only
Top Right *(Electric Bicycle Lamp Sign)* – Reference only
Bottom Left *(Advertising Sign)* – Reference only
Bottom Right *(Photograph)* – Reference only

PAGE 220

Top *(London Street Sign)* – $300+
Bottom Left *(Columbia Sign)* – $550
Bottom Right *(Columbia Sign)* – $450

PAGE 221

Top *(Steins)* – Reference only
Bottom Left *(Longines Watch Display)* – $250
Bottom Right *(Watches)* – Reference only

PAGE 222

Top *(Bike Radio)* – Rare
Bottom Left *(Store Display for Tires)* – $100
Bottom Right *(Store Display)* – $100

PAGE 223

Top *(Master Bike Locks)* – Reference only
Middle Left *(Whistles, Bells, etc.)* – Reference only
Middle Right *(Bike Lamps)* – Reference only
Bottom *(Badges)* – Reference only

PAGE 224

Top – $500
Bottom – $1000

PAGE 225

Top Left – $1000
Top Right – $1000
Bottom Left – $75
Bottom Right – $550

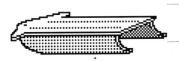

Riding Toys

WITH PRICE GUIDE
(No Pedal Cars)

Item # 1047

Included in this book are many color photos of **wagons, tricycles, scooters, sleds, irish mails, ride-ons, mobos, and rocking horses**. Covering pre 1900's to early 1900's and later. Many restored and many original riding toys. Also included in this book are many catalog pages for reference and pricing.

The price guide has current values. This is the book to price and identify your riding toys. A postcard section is also included in this book with a full color page of beautiful postcards.

The book is 8 1/2" x 11", softbound, and 194 pages, including catalog pages.
$29.95 + $2.00 shipping

SEND CHECK OR MONEY ORDER TO:
L-W BOOK SALES
P.O. Box 69 • Gas City, IN 46933

OR CALL:
1-800-777-6450
for **VISA, MASTERCARD** and **C.O.D.** orders only!!!
DEALERS CALL 1-317-674-6450 FOR FREE CATALOG AND INFORMATION

EVOLUTION OF THE
PEDAL CAR Vol. 1

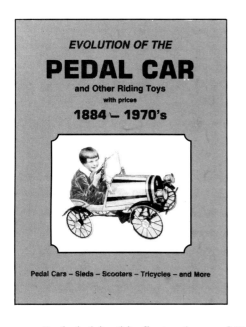

8 1/2" x 11"
Softbound
$29.95
with
Price Guide

Included in this first volume of Pedal Car books
re; 170 Actual Catalog pages from 1884 thru 1970's; and
00's of Pedal Cars and Riding Toys, many restored and
many originals.

EVOLUTION OF THE
PEDAL CAR Vol. 2

8 1/2" x 11"
Softbound
$29.95
with
Price Guide

MANY NEVER BEFORE SEEN PEDAL CARS!

This second volume of the Pedal Car books has over
200 pages, current prices, more catalog pages, and **no duplications** from book one. This book covers Pedal Cars from
Pre-1900's to 1980's.

EVOLUTION OF THE
PEDAL CAR Vol. 3

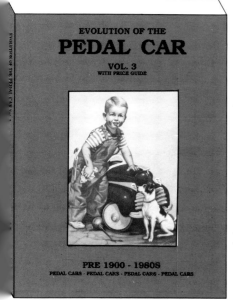

8 1/2" x 11"
Softbound
$29.95
with
Price Guide

MANY NEVER BEFORE SEEN PEDAL CARS!

This third volume of the Pedal Car books has over
0 pages, a postcard section, over 1000 cars priced, with
re actual old photographs, **and no duplications** from pre-
us volumes.

EVOLUTION OF THE
PEDAL CAR Vol. 4

8 1/2" x 11"
Softbound
$29.95
with
Price Guide

MANY NEVER BEFORE SEEN PEDAL CARS!

This fourth volume of the Pedal Car books has over
290 pages; lots of cars including their prices; with more
actual ads; a listing of contributors; dealers and restorers;
and no duplications from previous volumes.

SEND CHECK OR MONEY ORDERS TO: **L-W BOOK SALES • P.O. Box 69 • Gas City, IN 46933**

OR CALL FOR **VISA, MASTERCARD** or **C.O.D. ORDERS** • **1-800-777-6450**

FOR FREE CATALOG OR INFORMATION CALL: **1-317-674-6450**

Evolution of the
Bicycle
with price guide

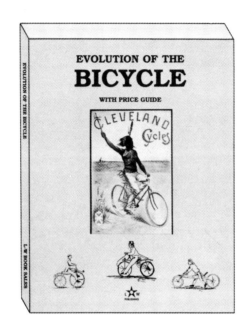

The Evolution of the Bicycle is a general price guide showing you the different types of bicycles dated from the 1850's to the 1960's. There are high-wheelers, custom built, classics, and boneshakers all included in this book. Over 1000 bikes illustrated and priced, many catalog pages, postcards, trade cards, and magazine ads also pictured.

8 1/2" x 11", Softbound and over 200 pages
$29.95 + $2.00 Shipping

Send a Check or money order to:
L-W BOOK SALES
P.O. Box 69 • Gas City, IN 46933

or calL for **VISA, MASTERCARD** or **C.O.D.** orders:
1-800-777-6450